The Gift of Flowers

Empower your life and energy with nature healing

CHERALYN DARCEY

ROCKPOOL
PUBLISHING

For Wendy and Bob,
neighbours who have grown
like wildflowers in my heart
to become loved and treasured friends.

A Rockpool book
PO Box 252
Summer Hill
NSW 2130
Australia
www.rockpoolpublishing.com.au
www.facebook.com/rockpoolpublishing

ISBN 978-1-925429-97-8

First published in 2019

This edition published in 2019

Design by Trenett Ha, Rockpool Publishing
Images by Shutterstock
Printed and bound in China

10 9 8 7 6 5 4 3 2 1

Contents

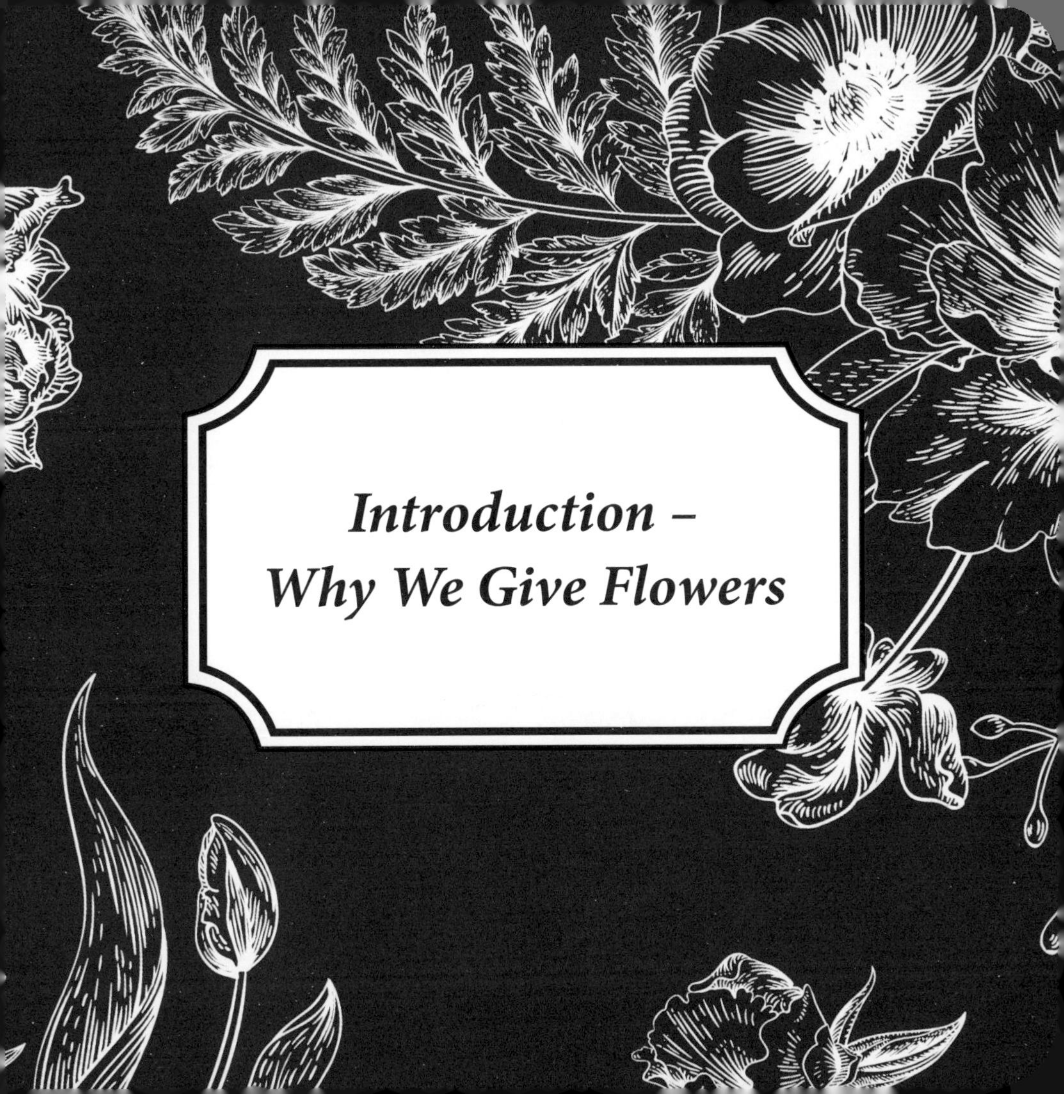

Introduction – Why We Give Flowers

In joy or sadness flowers are our constant friends.
– Okakura Kakuzo

We have always invited flowers into every facet of our lives. Flowers and the treasures they create, such as perfumes, foods and medicines, have been readily embraced for their supportive and healing attributes by us throughout time. They are our little friends who help us send messages, support and love to others, to the Gods and to ourselves. Flowers are usually with us when we are born, when we join our lives with another, when we celebrate, commiserate, placate and when we leave this earth, at which time we can be covered in flowers. The blossoms of plants

are with us always and they are a beautiful gift that illustrates and narrates our lives.

Archaeologists have discovered what appears to be the remnants of floral offerings within many ancient burial sites throughout the world. It is not hard for us to imagine that our ancestors would be moved to collect beautiful flowers from the forests, fields and hills surrounding them and place these colourful, sweet reminders of life with the departed for their journey elsewhere.

Some of the first recorded instances of the giving of flowers and the use of floral arrangements can be seen in the paintings, decorations and sculptures of the Ancient Egyptians. These were perhaps also our first 'cut-flower' gardeners, planting flowers and tending them for pleasure. The Egyptians of these times also believed that flowers held a sacred quality through not only their appearance but via their fragrances, and so flowers themselves, along with oils and perfumes, were used not only in daily life, but were an important element in religious ceremonies and rituals.

The flowers that seem to be most used by the Egyptians are the narcissus, blue scilla, delphinium, Siberian iris, rose and the lotus flower. There are many instances of floral offerings to deities being depicted but also those of people carrying flower bouquets and what clearly appear to be arranged flowers in temples, tombs and also in homes. It would seem that at first we gave flowers to the gods and then each other.

The Ancient Greeks and Romans held flowers in high regard as well, also adorning the statues of their deities in tribute during festivals and celebrations. These gifts of flowers to the gods and goddess by the Greeks, Romans and the Ancient Egyptians were perhaps the first indications of actual 'giving of flowers' to mark occasions and also in the gifting of flowers for pleasure. The act of giving flowers to a god or goddess was to appease, to make them happy. Surely we would suppose, even before this, in prehistoric times, humans might have been moved by some emotion to pluck and give a flower to another to cheer, to indicate interest or simply share the wonder of nature.

By the times of the Greeks and the Romans, military and sporting heroes where bestowed with wreaths, garlands and floral tributes to mark victories and fragrant petals showered from above to fill streets during these parades as well as during religious processions. Flowers abundantly decorated the homes, temples and public spaces of these lands for pleasure as well as spiritual reasons during festivals and special occasions, but they were increasingly becoming part of everyday life as people began giving flowers to each other.

Throughout Ancient Asia, flowers were an important element in the home and at temples, where their main function was to offer protection from evil spirits. Taoists and Buddhists lay flowers at their altars as offerings and have done so for centuries. Plants and their flowers have been integral to healing medicine and rituals in most Asian countries and these practices have flourished along with spiritual and decorative uses that still hold great meaning and appreciation of nature and flowers.

As history moved forward, these ancient practices remained, and with the birth of Christianity, flowers were also used as decorations and were aligned with different religious figures, festivals and occasions of Christian beliefs. In the 16th century we see the use of flowers within the church flourish with roses and lilies, flowers symbolic of purity, innocence and love, holding great favour for brides, funerals and occasions celebrating the Virgin Mary and the Resurrection of Christ.

During the Middle Ages, magick, superstition and folklore thrived, and we still see many of these traditions today. Theatre was popular and superstitions numerous, including the belief that any flowers on the stage would be unlucky. The only way to counter this was to present them at the end of the production to the leading lady and this would actually confer good luck upon the play and cast. This began the tradition of us giving flowers to someone who had performed or done well.

Valentine's Day, 14th February, is perhaps the best-known day of flower giving throughout the world when we show

others that they are loved by us. During his reign in third century Rome, the Emperor Claudius I believed that soldiers were better at their job if they remained single, so he made marrying illegal for them. A young priest named Valentine defied the law and secretly married young couples; however, he was discovered and sentenced to death. While incarcerated, Valentine fell in love with the jailer's daughter and before he was executed on 14th February in 270 AD, he wrote her a letter and signed it, 'from your Valentine.' He was declared a saint and we still honour his commitment to love (even unwittingly) by gifting flowers and other tokens of love to those we hold dear.

There are many other beautiful traditions of flower-giving throughout time and across all cultures with most beginning as offerings to the gods and goddesses of various faiths and then becoming ways to honour and celebrate our family, friends, loved ones and the places we find ourselves living, working and enjoying life in. Although these grander and commemorative gestures can be traced through our cultures, the simple act of enjoying something ourselves and delighting in the act of sharing with another is surely where the act of giving flowers began. We may have gathered the floral jewels of the fields for our gods but we would most certainly also have plucked the single blossom along the road to visit someone we loved and shared the happiness.

What Does Your Favourite Flower Say About You?

Perhaps your favourite flower, or one you are drawn to at the moment, is saying something about you.

Frangipani (*Plumeria alba*)

Those who love these summer-heralding flowers are freedom seekers and generally love the bright and colourful side of life. Warm-hearted, fun and beautiful people, inside and out, you will find they also adore travel. Frangipani will be telling you to look for the beauty and good within and that perhaps you need a little more space right now.

Sweet Pea (*Lathyrus odoratus*)

The comfort-lovers of the flower world, Sweet Pea folk adore the gorgeous, sumptuous and, at times, the luxurious. They are also very generous people who adore sharing and love seeing others they care about as contented as they need to be. Sweet Pea means you need to enjoy yourself more and to find some pleasure and relaxation.

Rose (*Rosa spp.*)

Rose people are usually romantics but also traditionalists at heart. History, the building of a legacy, old-fashioned romance and reverence for customs and traditions are all very precious to rose-lovers. Having a new or sudden desire for these blossoms indicates a focus on romance but also for grounding and an exploration of purpose and who you truly are.

Magnolia (*Magnolia spp.*)

The wisdom-seekers and keepers, Magnolia-lovers are usually keen researchers, readers and teachers. They have a reverence for truth and fairness and find a calling in knowledge along with a never-ending dedication to sharing it. Magnolia calls to those who need to seek their personal truths and perhaps look more closely at their goals and where they are currently heading.

Peony (*Paeonia officinalis*)

Peony people are natural healers and are especially adept with complementary modalities. They are also very keen on creating beautiful spaces (they love art!), being of service and looking after others, especially those in need and animals. Being drawn to Peony usually means you need to look after your own needs and health a little more closely.

Tulip (*Tulipa spp.*)

Desire, passion, attraction; these are all themes of Tulips and those who love them will usually find themselves driven a little harder than those around them to succeed. The entrepreneurs of the flower world who usually do well wherever they find themselves. Tulips reach out to those needing a boost in confidence and in self-belief.

Sunflower (*Helianthus annuus*)

Sunflower people are usually strong, resilient, warm and very compassionate. Creativity, especially that which can enhance their surrounds, appeals to them greatly and they are often found working in the arts and crafts world. If you have a desire to surround yourself with Sunflowers then you are needing strength, perhaps some courage and a boost in happiness.

Lily (*Lilium spp.*)

The great protectors are our Lily-lovers. They are the eco-warriors, the law keepers and makers, the healers too and those who are working hard to make the world a better place. You will find they are usually encouraging, supportive and very caring. Desiring Lilies is to want added protection and also indicates a promise to be made or kept.

Orchid (*Orchidaceae spp.*)

Those who adore Orchids are among the most unique of people. They are very dedicated and passionate and are driven in some way with their focus. Unusual in their tastes and their lifestyles, they are incredibly interesting and usually very intelligent. A desire for Orchids is an indication of wanting more out of life than is currently on offer.

Don't like a flower?

It may mean you don't have time for: Frangipani – fickleness, Sweet Pea – laziness, Rose – rules, Magnolia – tradition, Peony – pampering, Tulip – enthusiasm, Sunflower – optimism, Lily – fate, Orchid – mystery.

The Nourishing Gift of Flowers

Flowers always make people better, happier, and more helpful; they are sunshine, food and medicine to the soul.
– Luther Burbank

Blossoms are not only beautiful, many are also tasty, nutritious and can fill you with their energetic goodness. While you can, and should, try growing them for yourself, these days you will find suppliers, growers and stores sharing edible flowers amongst the fruit and vegetables. Have a look in your area, as there are even specialists that have made edible blossoms their only or main business, such is the growing popularity and

interest in flower feasting. Not all flowers are edible, and some are not safe, so be sure you identify correctly and only ever eat organic.

You can easily add flowers that are edible to your existing recipes, especially salads and sandwiches, and naturally they make delightful and yummy decorations for finger foods and sweet treats. The energetic qualities of flowers will also be imparted when using them in your foods so check The Language of Flowers lists in the Flower Lore chapter later in this book. Nasturtiums (Tropaeolum majus), for example, have a zesty pepper-like flavour that makes a sandwich or salad zing, but they may also give you added vitality, confidence and a boost in creative thinking. Sprinkle pretty and nectar-sweet Heartease (Viola tricolor), over your desserts, drinks and vegetable dishes to impart peace of mind, to comfort and to add an element of merriment.

The Flavours of Edible Flowers

These are just some of the many edible blossoms and their flavours. Ensure that only organic and properly identified flowers and their parts are used. As a rule, only the outer 'petals' (usually the bracts) should be used of flowers deemed edible, and this is especially true of composite flowers (those that consist of many tiny flowers on a main flower head). The tiny inner flowers can cause skin irritation and even an allergic reaction in some individuals.

- **Angelica** (*Angelica archangelica*) celery
- **Anise Hyssop** (*Agastache foeniculum*) licorice
- **Apple** (*Malus spp*) light floral
- **Arugula** (*Eruca vesicaria*) spicy
- **Basil** (*Ocimum basilicum*) aromatic, slightly sweet
- **Bee Balm** (*Monarda spp.*) Earl Grey tea
- **Borage** (*Borago officinalis*) light cucumber
- **Calendula** (*Calendula officinalis*) tangy, spicy, pepper
- **Carnation** (*Dianthus caryophyllus*) cloves, spicy
- **Chamomile** (*Chamaemelum nobile*) light apple
- **Chicory** (*Cichorium intybus*) endive
- **Chives** (*Allium schoenoprasum*) slight onion

- **Chrysanthemum** (*Chrysanthemum coronarium*) bitter
- **Lemon** *(Citrus limon)* very strong waxy lemon
- **Clover** (*Trifolium spp.*) sweet nectar if picked early
- **Coriander** (*Coriander sativum*) pungent
- **Cornflower** (*Centaurea cynaus*) clove, sweet and spicy
- **Dandelion** (*Taraxacum officinale*) mushroom, earthy
- **Elderflower** (*Sambucus nigra*) sweet
- **English Daisy** (*Bellis perennis*) tangy
- **Fennel** (*Foeniculum vulgare*) sweet licorice
- **Fuchsia** (*Fuchsia spp.*) tart
- **Gardenia** (*Gardenia jasminoides*) sweet, perfumy
- **Garlic Chives** (*Allium tuberosum*) garlic
- **Gladiolus** (*Gladiolus spp.*) lettuce
- **Heartsease** (*Viola tricolor*) nectar, sweet
- **Hibiscus** (*Hibiscus rosa-sinensis*) tart
- **Hollyhock** (*Alcea rosea*) bland
- **Impatiens** (*Impatiens walleriana*) bland

- **Jasmine, Arabian** (*Jasminum sambac*) light sweet
- **Johnny-Jump-Up** (*Viola tricolor*) mild sweet
- **Lavender** (*Lavandula spp.*) perfumy
- **Lemon Verbena** (*Aloysia triphylla*) lemon
- **Lilac** (*Syringa vulgaris*) floral, lemon
- **Mallow** (*Malva sylvestris*) light sweet
- **Marigold, Signet** (*Tagetes tenuifolia*) spicy
- **Marjoram** (*Origanum majorana*) mild marjoram
- **Mint** (*Mentha spp.*) mild mint
- **Nasturtium** (*Tropaeolum majus*) peppery, sweet
- **Orchid** (*Dendrobium spp.*) slightly bitter
- **Pansy** (*Viola x wittrockiana*) tart, sweet
- **Pea** (*Pisum spp.*) mild sweet
- **Primrose** (*Primula vulgaris*) sweet
- **Radish** (*Raphanus sativus*) mild, sweet radish
- **Rose** (*R. gallica officinalis*) sweet, aromatic
- **Rosemary** (*Rosmarinus officinalis*) savory, pine

- **Runner Bean** (*Phaseolus coccineus*) mild bean, sweet, nectar
- **Safflower** (*Carthamus tinctorius*) mild saffron
- **Sage** (*Salvia officinalis*) mild version of leaves
- **Scented Geranium** (*Pelargonium spp.*) honey, lemon, mint
- **Snapdragon** (*Antirrhinum majus*) tart, very bitter
- **Society Garlic** (*Tulbaghia violacea*) mild garlic
- **Squash Blossom** (*Cucurbita pepo spp.*) honey, sweet
- **Sunflower** (*Helianthus annuus*) light bitter
- **Thyme** (*Thymus vulgaris*) light lemon
- **Violet** (*Viola odorata*) light sweet
- **Violet, Native** (*Viola hederacea*) sweet

Never Eat These Flowers

A short list of just some popular flowers that are poisonous and must never be eaten or used in or near foods. Always check with a reputable authority as to the suitability of a flower for culinary use and for its accurate identification.

- **Azalea** *Rhododendron spp.*
- **Buttercup** *Ranunculus spp.*
- **Daffodil** *Narcissus spp.*
- **Delphinium** *Delphinium spp.*
- **Four o' clock** *Mirabilis jalapa*
- **Foxglove** *Digitalis purpurea*
- **Hyacinth** *Hyacinthus orientalis*
- **Hydrangea** *Hydrangea spp.*
- **Iris** *Iris spp.*
- **Jonquil** *Narcissus spp.*
- **Lantana** *Lantana camara*
- **Lily of the valley** *Convallaria majalis*
- **Morning glory** *Ipomoea violacea*
- **Oleander** *Nerium oleander*

- **Periwinkle** *Vinca spp.*
- **Philodendron** *Philodendron spp.*
- **Sweet pea** *Lathyrus spp.*
- **Wisteria** *Wisteria spp.*
- **Yesterday-today-and-tomorrow** *Brunfelsia spp.*

Grow a Flower Feast Salad Booster Planter Box

This box could be mounted to a window that enjoys full sun throughout the day or placed in a sunny spot in your garden, balcony or courtyard. All are easy to maintain plants that will give salads a yummy and lovely floral boost. Pick as flowers bloom, wash well, chop and toss into your salads and salad fillings in wraps and sandwiches. Grow organic; to do this, look out for organic potting mix, and only use organic pest control and fertilisers. Any edible flowers could be grown, but try these for an easy start: Chives, Borage, Native Violet, Nasturtium, Basil.

Flower Food and Drink Recipes

One of the most attractive things about the flowers is their beautiful reserve.
– Henry David Thoreau

Blossom Risotto

Serves 4

This delicious and nutritious rice-based dish is also a delight on the dinner table with its kaleidoscope of floral goodness. Select a brilliant mixture of petals or perhaps one type of flower to impart the energy you desire.

You will need

- 2 leeks
- 2 - 4 cloves garlic (to taste)
- 2 tablespoons olive oil
- 2 tablespoons butter

- 2 cups Arborio rice
- up to 4 cups of warm stock (vegetable or meat)
- 1 cup white wine*
- 1 tablespoon fresh thyme leaves
- 1 cup finely grated parmesan (optional)
- a good handful of chopped edible flowers/petals

To make

Finely chop all the white and a little of the green of your leek and sauté in the oil over a medium heat until translucent. Finely chop the garlic and add, cooking for another few minutes, constantly stirring. Reduce the heat, add the butter and then the Arborio rice and finely chopped thyme. Pour in the wine/stock substitution and stir constantly while the rice absorbs all the liquid. Keep adding stock slowly and stirring constantly until the rice is cooked. You will want a creamy texture and the rice to be cooked to your liking. Take off the heat and stir in your flowers/petals and, if desired, grated parmesan.

*additional stock can be substituted for wine

With freedom, books, flowers, and the moon,
who could not be happy?
– Oscar Wilde

Borage and Nasturtium Fritters

Serves 4

A really delicious all-day breakfast favourite made floral-wonderful with the addition of purple borage and sunny nasturtiums. You can substitute these blossoms for other edible flowers, just watch the flavours as more savoury flavours will work best.

You will need

- 1 cup self-raising flour
- 2 eggs
- 1/3 cup milk
- 2 cans corn kernels (400g)
- 100g fetta
- 1 tablespoon butter

- a dash of olive oil
- 2 tablespoons chopped borage flowers
- 1 tablespoon chopped borage leaves
- 2 tablespoons chopped nasturtium petals

To make

Sift the flour into a large mixing bowl. In a separate bowl, whisk together the eggs and the milk and then pour slowly into the flour, stirring constantly until well combined. Drain the corn and add along with fetta, flowers and leaves. Melt butter and olive oil in a large frypan and create the fritters by dropping ¼ cup sized balls into pan. Flatten to about 2cm and cook until golden. Flip to cook through other side. Serve with your selection of lemon wedges, sweet chilli sauce, hummus or smashed avocado.

People from a planet without flowers would think we must be mad with joy the whole time to have such things about us.
– Iris Murdoch

Purple Petal Fizz

Serves 4

A selection of flowers that traditionally impart feelings of protection, moving on and peace-making go together to create this wonderful bubbly beverage to celebrate endings or new beginnings.

You will need

- 3 teaspoons lavender flower heads
- 2 teaspoons violet petals
- ½ cup lilac petals
- ½ cup water
- 2 teaspoons rosewater
- a bottle of champagne, sparkling wine or mineral water
- a glass jug
- a few additional flower petals to serve

To make

Place the flowers and petals into a pan and stir in water. Bring to a gentle boil and lower temperature to a simmer for a few minutes. Keep watch and, when the petals are translucent, remove from heat and strain. Cool this liquid and refrigerate until very cold. When ready to serve, add to jug along with rosewater and champagne/sparkling wine or mineral water. Pour into champagne glasses and top with a few flower petals.

Flowers enshrine my heart between their petals; that's why my heartbeats love them so much.
– Munia Khan

Flower Power Vinegar

Makes approximately 1 cup

Use this flower vinegar in any recipe that you would regular vinegars. It is especially good as a salad dressing, especially for salads you create with flowers. Other edible flowers can be substituted for those listed in this recipe. Straining the mixture is optional or you may like to add additional fresh flower petals to your bottled vinegars once complete.

You will need

- a sterilised jar with lid, approximately 3 cups in size
- ½ cup chrysanthemum petals
- ½ cup geranium petals
- ½ cup rose petals
- 1 cup white wine vinegar
- ½ teaspoon sugar
- a pinch of salt
- sterilised jar or bottle for storage

To make

Place the petals into your sterilised jar. Gently warm the petals over a low heat but do not boil; remove from the heat and stir in the sugar and salt. Pour over the petals. Close the lid and shake well. Leave for a few days in a sunny position, shaking regularly. Once the petals become translucent, strain into the storage jar or bottle. Your flower vinegar is ready and can be used in cooking wherever vinegar is called for.

A flower blossoms for its own joy.
– Oscar Wilde

Flower-infused Oil

Makes 1 cup

Flavoured oils can be created with herbs and spices, but this lovely oil is infused with flowers. You can use the oil in any place that you would use regular oils, although do not employ high heats or frying methods as it will destroy the flavours. Straining the mixture is optional.

You may like to add additional fresh flower petals to your bottled vinegars once complete.

You will need

- 1 cup mild olive oil or coconut oil (other food oils can be used)
- ¼ cup fresh or dried edible flower petals
- a double boiler or two saucepans that nest
- water
- a fine strainer

- a sterilised bottle/s for storage

To make

Chop or crush flower petals. Set up your double boiler or place a smaller saucepan into a larger one. Pour enough water into the lower saucepan so that the water level comes up to about half the height of the inner saucepan. If using coconut oil, warm very gently until melted. If using olive oil, heat gently until warm. Add the flower petals and gently simmer for five minutes. Remove from heat, cover and let steep for an hour. Strain into the storage jar or bottle. Store in a cool, dry and dark place. Should be used within 12 months unopened and three months once opened.

I count my blessings with the flowers, never
with the leaves that fall.
– Lady Bird Johnson

'Goodnight Petal' Sleep Tea

Serves one

A gently calming and delicious tea is enhanced with flower petals to bring you a good night's sleep. Make and drink about an hour before bedtime. If you cannot find rooibos tea, use two teaspoons of chamomile tea.

You will need

- 1 cup of milk or milk substitute
- 1 small cinnamon stick
- 1 cardamom pod
- 1 teaspoon chopped valerian root
- 1 teaspoon of rooibos tea leaves
- a few drops of pure vanilla extract
- ¼ teaspoon ground nutmeg
- 1 teaspoon chamomile tea
- honey to sweeten
- mortar and pestle or spice grinder

- fine strainer
- saucepan

To make

This recipe makes a cup for one person, so increase amounts as needed to serve more of the family. Perhaps you could make a lovely big pot for everyone before bedtime.

Grind the cinnamon and cardamom. Place the milk, nutmeg, chamomile tea/rooibos tea and valerian into a saucepan. Add the cinnamon and cardamom and bring to a simmer for five minutes, but do not allow to boil. Remove from heat, strain and pour into a cup. Add the vanilla extract and stir in honey (amount to your taste). Drink before bed.

Sometimes the tiniest flowers smell
the sweetest.
– Emilie Barnes

Traditional Elderflower Cordial

Makes about 1.5 litres/3 pints

A beautiful summer cordial that can be used in chilled still or sparkling water, as a cocktail addition, in desert cooking or drizzled over ice-creams and sorbets.

You will need

- 15 heads of elderflower
- 2 cups white sugar
- 6 cups of water
- 4 tablespoons citric acid*
- 6 medium-sized lemons

To make

Boil the water. Into a large heatproof bowl, place the sugar and then pour in the boiling water. Stir well until all the sugar has dissolved. Let cool. Wash and dry all lemons. Finely grate the skins of two lemons and then thickly slice them. Remove skin of remaining four lemons, thickly slice and discard skins.

Add the grated lemon skin and lemon slices, along with citric acid to the mixture. Next add the Elderflowers and stir well. Cover the bowl with a clean cloth and leave in a cool place so the mixture can steep for 48 hours. Strain through an ultra-fine sieve or a muslin cloth into a jug.

Bottle in sterilised glass bottle/s. You may need to use a funnel. Unopened, this will keep in a cool, dark place for a month; unopened in the fridge, it will keep for three months, but once opened, use within two weeks. Can be frozen for up to six months.

*Citric acid can be replaced with the same quantity of a thin honey.

Violets smell like burnt sugar cubes that have been dipped in lemon and velvet.
– Diane Ackerman

Violet Honey

Makes 2 cups

This honey will add a lovely sweet floral note to drinks, foods and cooking. An added benefit of this flower and honey mixture is that it is very good for sore throats. Let a teaspoon dissolve in your mouth to sooth and calm any inflammation.

You will need

- 2 cups of mild organic honey
- a handful of violet petals (*Viola odorata*)
- a double boiler or two saucepans that nest
- water
- a fine strainer
- a sterilised jar/s

To make

Set up your double boiler or place a smaller saucepan into a larger one. Pour enough water into the lower saucepan so that

the water level comes up to about half the height of the inner saucepan. Place the honey and the violet petals into the inside saucepan and warm very gently on a low heat for five minutes. Strain into sterilised jar/s. Store in a cool dry and dark place and use within 12 months, and within a month once opened.

Life is the flower for which love is the honey.
– Victor Hugo

Chamomile Honey Teacake

Serves 8

A pretty and sweet teacake, perfect to share with family and friends for morning or afternoon tea, that you can decorate with additional edible flowers if you desire. You could use the Violet Honey in the previous recipe in place of plain honey to drizzle.

You will need

- 2 tablespoons chamomile tea
- ¾ cup room temperature butter
- ¾ cup caster sugar
- 1 teaspoon vanilla extract
- 2 eggs
- 1 and ¼ cups self-raising flour
- ¼ cup plain flour
- ½ cup full cream milk
- ¼ cup honey

To make

Preheat the oven to 180C/160C Fan, 350/320F. Grease and line a 20cm/8in cake tin with baking paper. Using a spice grinder or a mortar and pestle, grind the chamomile tea until very fine. In a large bowl, beat the butter, sugar and vanilla together until creamy, either by hand or with a mixer. Add the eggs, one at a time, and ensure you beat very well after each addition. Sift the self-raising and plain flours into the bowl along with the ground chamomile tea. Fold in the milk gently and mix well. Spread into the cake tin evenly. Bake for 60 minutes or until skewer inserted into the centre comes out clean. Let cool for 10 to 15 minutes in the tin and then turn out onto a wire rack. When completely cooled, drizzle with honey.

Take time to smell the roses.
Proverb

Rose Petal Sugar

Makes 2 cups

You can use any edible flowers and even combinations to create this very handy natural sweetener. It can be used just as you would use plain sugar in your drinks and cooking, and for those people who love creating cocktails, this would make a very interesting ingredient in your concoctions.

You will need

- 2 cups of edible rose petals
- 1 cup sugar
- a sterilised jar/s

To make

Preheat oven to 120°C/250°F. Line a baking tray with baking paper. Grind up the rose petals and the sugar in small batches together, using either a mortar and pestle or a spice grinder. Lay the mixture out on the baking tray and bake for two hours. Remove from oven and smash up, grinding again if you desire a finer mixture. Store in sterilised jar/s in a cool, dry and dark place. Use with 12 months.

The Beauty Gifts
of Flowers

If you tend to a flower, it will bloom, no matter how many weeds surround it.
– Matshona Dhliwayo

Flowers have been used in beauty routines since ancient times. Roses in many forms were incredibly popular with the Romans and Greeks. They created rose oils and waters that were used as perfumes, cosmetics and beauty mixtures. The Ancient Egyptians not only created their own beauty products, they traded the ingredients and products with other countries. Most of these blends were based on plants and their flowers and their recipes were passed down throughout history. In Asia, flowers have been

used in cosmetics and skin care for centuries. Coloured lip balms - what we would think of today as lipstick or lip gloss - was once made with safflowers.

Pamper yourself and those you love with holistic treasures made from flowers. They will not only impart therapeutic qualities which will support and enhance you physically, but the flowers will also lend their fragrances and energies to fill your soul with calm, joy and sometimes zinging energy.

Create a Flower Spa Home Apothecary

There are a few basic ingredients that are used in many home spa preparations and so you may wish to collect them to have on hand and help you to build a base for your flower spa creations.

- Apple Cider Vinegar
- Beeswax
- Bicarbonate of Soda
- Castile Soap
- Cocoa Butter

- Essential Oils
- Kaolin Clay
- Oats
- Sea Salt
- Shea Butter
- Vegetable Glycerine
- Vegetable Wax
- Witch Hazel
- Carrier Oils (see list below)

You can use a selection of a few of these oils to provide the base for many spa and beauty preparations. You may substitute most for each other in many of the spa recipes that follow.

- Almond Oil
- Apricot Kernel Oil
- Argan Oil
- Avocado Oil
- Beeswax

- Castor Oil
- Coconut Oil
- Grapeseed Oil
- Jojoba Oil
- Macadamia Oil
- Neem Oil
- Olive Oil
- Rose Hip Oil
- Vitamin E Oil
- Wheat Germ Oil

Allergy Testing

Not all flowers are suitable to use topically (on your skin). You must perform a skin allergy test first before using any creation by dabbing a small pea-sized amount in the crook of your elbow and waiting for 24 hours to ensure there is no indication of possible allergy. This will include redness, itching and irritation.

The Qualities of Spa and Beauty Flowers

Flowers have many therapeutic and cosmetic qualities; to get you started, here is a selection of perhaps some of the most common flowers used in beauty and spa mixtures and some of the qualities and benefits they can impart.

Bergamot (*Monarda spp.*): hair strength, astringent, toning

Burdock (*Arctium spp.*): cleansing

Carnation (*Dianthus caryophyllus*): muscle soothing

Comfrey (*Symphytum officinale*): regeneration, inflammation reduction, healing, soothing

Chamomile, German (*Matricaria recutita*): hair lightener, anti-aging, wrinkle reduction, sensitive skin support, reduces puffiness, anti-inflammatory

Cone Flower (*Echinacea spp.*): exfoliant, soothing, hair health

Cornflower (*Centaurea cyanus*): healing

Dandelion (*Taraxacum officinale*): anti-aging, inflammation

reduction, detox, collagen stimulation

Elderflower (*Sambucus nigra*): softening, astringent, cleansing

Hibiscus (*Hibiscus rosa-sinensis*): anti-oxidant, exfoliant, toning, hydrating

Hyssop (*Hyssopus officinalis*): healing

Jasmine (*Jasminum officinale*): hydrating, cleansing, softening

Lady's Mantle (*Alchemilla vulgaris*): tightens pores, toning, anti-wrinkle

Lavender (*Lavandula spp.*): antiseptic, skin and mind soothing, oil balancer, healing

Lemon Balm (*Melissa officinalis*): toning, astringent

Lime (*Tilia x europaea*): astringent, wrinkle reduction, cleansing

Lotus (*Nelumbo nucifera*): soothing, antioxidant, hydrating, improves elasticity, anti-aging

Marigold (*Calendula officinalis*): soothing, healing

Mullein (*Verbascum thapsus*): soothing, healing

Nasturtium (*Tropaeolum majus*): antiseptic

Orchid (*Orchidaceae spp.*): renewal, hydrating

Pansy (*Viola tricolor var. hortensis*): astringent, emollient

Passion flower (*Passiflora incarnata*): calming, soothing, anti-aging, protection

Rose (*Rosa spp.*): softener, hydrator, astringent, calms redness

Sunflower (*Helianthus annuus*): healing

Tansy (*Tanacetum vulgare*): healing, cleansing

Violet (*Viola odorata*): cleansing, soothing, astringent

Wallflower (*Cheiranthus cheiri*): muscle relaxant, nerve-soothing

Wild Geranium (*Geranium maculatum*): astringent, toning, inflammation reduction, antibacterial, cell regeneration

Yarrow (*Achillea millefolium*): oil reducer for hair or skin

Spa and Beauty Recipes

The splendour of the rose and the whiteness
of the lily do not rob the little violet of its scent
nor the daisy of its simple charm.
– Therese of Lisieux

Violet and Carnation Face Cleanser

Makes approximately 1 cup

An effective and gentle facial cleanser that can be used daily as the start of a beautiful flower-filled natural beauty routine. To use, massage into face and then rinse.

You will need

- 2 cups of water
- 1 cup milk
- ½ cup violets (*Viola odorata*)
- ½ cup carnation petals (*Dianthus caryophyllus*)
- saucepan

- a smaller glass/Pyrex/ceramic bowl
- blender
- sterilised bottle

To make

Boil the water and then remove from heat. Place the smaller bowl within the saucepan of hot water, and then pour in milk and add the violet flowers and the carnation petals. Cover bowl and let stand for 15 mins until the milk is warm. Pour mixture into blender and blend until you attain a smooth consistency. Store in the refrigerator in sterilised bottle and use within seven days.

Every flower is a soul blossoming in nature.
– Gérard de Nerval

Golden Marigold Facial Toner

Makes 1 cup

Create this toner and add it to your daily skin care ritual to even out the texture of your skin and impart soothing healing as well. To use, shake the bottle well and use a cotton pad/ball to apply by dabbing over face after cleansing. Don't rinse.

You will need

- 1 cup water
- ¼ cup marigold petals (*Calendula officinalis*)
- 1 tablespoon honey
- 2 drops lavender essential oil
- 1 tablespoon apple cider vinegar
- heat-proof bowl
- mixing bowl
- whisk
- cloth

- fine strainer
- sterilised bottle/s

To make

Boil the water and pour into heat-proof glass or ceramic bowl. Add the Marigold petals and stir, cover with the cloth and leave to cool for at least 30 minutes. Pour the honey, lavender essential oil and apple cider vinegar into the mixing bowl and then whisk until all very well combined. Strain the flower water into this mixture and stir. Bottle in sterilised bottle/s. This recipe will keep for a week unrefrigerated, but is best stored in the fridge, where it will keep for six weeks.

There are always flowers for those who want to see them.
- Henri Matisse

Magnolia Moisturiser

Makes approximately ½ cup

The essential oils that I have used here are my favourites for this blend, but you can use any of your favourites that are suitable for use on the face and body. To use, massage into the face/body after cleansing morning and night.

You will need

- ½ cup shea butter
- ¼ cup magnolia petals
- 2 tablespoons olive oil
- 8 drops lavender essential oil
- 4 drops magnolia essential oil
- blender
- a double boiler or two saucepans you can nest
- a wooden spoon
- sterilised jar/s
- whisk

To make

Make sure that magnolia petals are clean and completely dry. Blend the magnolia petals until they are smooth. Place the shea butter into the double boiler and melt over a low heat. Remove from the heat and add the olive oil. Place in the refrigerator for about 30 minutes until the mixture becomes solid, but do not allow it to become hard. Add the lavender and magnolia essential oils and the magnolia petal paste. Whisk until the mixture is a smooth and creamy consistency. Store at room temperature in sterilised jar/s. Use within a month.

Flowers don't worry about how they're going to bloom. They just open up and turn toward the light and that makes them beautiful.
– Jim Carrey

Rose Rejuvenation Face Oil

Makes approximately ½ cup

This rose-infused elixir will create a gorgeous rich beauty rejuvenation oil. This mixture will keep best in a dark-coloured glass bottle or jar. Use nightly after cleansing as a healing supporter of your skin's regenerative processes that occur while you are sleeping. For skin that it is particularly dry, you can use lightly before moisturising each morning.

You will need

- petals of one red Rose (*Rosa spp.*)
- 8 tablespoons of almond oil
- 3 tablespoons of vitamin E oil
- 8 drops of rose essential oil
- cheesecloth or muslin cloth
- two sterilised glass bottles

To make

Place the red rose petals and the oils into the sterilised glass bottle, and seal with lid. Place in a dark, cool cupboard for three days. Gently shake once or twice a day. Take the bottle out after three days and strain the mixture through the cloth into the other sterilised bottle. Store in a cool dry place out of direct light. Can be decanted into smaller bottles. Use within three months.

All the flowers of the tomorrows are in the seeds of today.
– Indian Proverb

Gardenia Clay Face Mask

Makes ½ cup

A deep cleansing and moisture-balancing facial mask enhanced with the rejuvenating qualities of Gardenia. This recipe will create one application and is best used immediately. Spread over clean dry skin. Leave for an hour and then rinse off. Splash face with cold water to close pores.

You will need

- ¼ cup kaolin
- ¼ cup spring water
- 6 dried Gardenia flower petals (*Gardenia jasminoides*)
- glass or ceramic bowl

To make

Place kaolin clay into the bowl and then crush the Gardenia petals over the clay and mix well. Pour the water over the top and mix. Cover and let stand for an hour before use.

A flower's appeal is in its contradictions – so delicate in form yet strong in fragrance, so small in size yet big in beauty, so short in life yet long on effect.

– Terri Guillemets

Floral Hair Rinse

Creates approximately 1 cup

These lively flower water rinses will impart shine and strength to your hair. Select the flowers that are best suited to your hair type and pour over hair after washing and conditioning. Work through with your fingers and leave on for three minutes. Rinse, dry and style as usual.

You will need

- 1 cup boiling water
- 1 tablespoon flower petals
- glass/Pyrex/ceramic bowl with cover/lid
- wooden spoon
- fine mesh strainer
- sterilised bottle or jar

To make

Place the flower petals into the bowl and pour in the boiling water. Mix gently with the wooden spoon and then cover. Leave until completely cool. Strain into sterilised bottle or jar. Keep refrigerated for up to a week. This mixture makes one application.

Fair hair: Use Chamomile, Marigold or Yarrow

Dark hair: Use Rosemary or Sage (flowers/leaves)

Even the tiniest of flowers can have the toughest roots.
– Shannon M Mullen

Apple Blossom Lip Balm

Makes approximately ¼ cup

This lovely soothing balm will keep your lips soft and add a little gloss. It is also very healing for those that have dry lips. To use, spread a little on your lips as often as you wish.

You will need

- 1 tablespoon of coconut oil
- 1 tablespoon of coconut butter
- 1 teaspoon of vitamin E oil
- 3 apple spice herbal teabags
- ¼ teaspoon of raw sugar
- ¼ teaspoon of vanilla extract
- 2 tablespoons of beeswax pellets
- a double boiler or two saucepans you can nest
- a wooden spoon
- 1 or 2 tiny sterilised containers suitable for lip balm

To make

Fill the outer double boiler (or alternate) with water up to the half-way mark of the inner vessel. Heat gently but do not allow to simmer or boil. Then add the coconut oil, coconut butter and vitamin E oil to the inner vessel, while stirring with the wooden spoon. Add the apple teabags, raw sugar and vanilla extract and keep stirring until the sugar dissolves. Take off the heat and leave to steep for five minutes. Once cool enough to handle, gently squeeze the teabags into the mixture, and then remove them. Place back on the heat and add the beeswax pellets. Stir until melted and well combined. Pour into containers for use. Use within three months.

Open the bloom of your heart and become a gift of beauty to the world.
– Bryant McGill

Rose Geranium Body Mousse

Makes approximately ½ cup

This flower-infused mousse will provide deep moisturising benefits, and with the addition of lavender it is also very relaxing. Use it after showering and bathing, smoothing into skin in circular motions.

You will need

- 2 tablespoons coconut oil
- 5 tablespoons unrefined shea butter
- 3 tablespoons almond oil
- 20 drops rose geranium essential oil
- a double boiler or two saucepans you can nest
- wooden spoon
- an electric mixer
- 6 heads of dried lavender (*Lavandula spp.*)
- mixing bowl
- sterilised jar/s

To make

Melt the coconut oil and shea butter in the double boiler while constantly stirring gently with a wooden spoon. Remove from the heat once melted, and then stir in the almond oil. Leave to cool until any trace of heat has dissipated - this will take a couple of hours, depending on your location and conditions. Stir in the essential oil. Using an electric mixer, whip mixture for three minutes. Place in the refrigerator for 24 hours. Finely crush dried lavender flowers and then fold into mixture. Whip again for another three minutes and then place in sterilised jar/s.

To be overcome by the fragrance of flowers is
a delectable form of defeat.
– Beverley Nichols

Flower Perfume Balm

Makes approximately 5 tablespoons

This solid perfume can be set in wearable lockets or small containers that you can carry with you. They make delightful gifts and can be created with a variety of essential oils and flower petals to blend your very own fragrances. To use, dab a little on pulse points. Use within six months.

You will need

- 2 tablespoon beeswax pellets
- 3 tablespoons sweet almond oil
- 20 drops essential oil
- a double boiler or two saucepans you can nest
- wooden stirrer
- glass measuring cup
- small containers or lockets
- flower petals

To make

Place the beeswax pellets into the double boiler and melt over a low heat. Do not leave alone as beeswax can easily overheat and catch fire, and remove from heat as soon as melted. Add the sweet almond oil and your selected essential oils and flower petals. Stir with wooden stirrer. Pour into the glass measuring jug and then quickly pour into lockets or small containers. Leave to set

Suggested blends

Rose Garden

- 6 drops rose essential oil
- 5 drops bergamot essential oil
- ½ teaspoon finely crushed dried rose petals

Jasmine Nights

- 6 drops jasmine essential oil
- 4 drops vanilla essential oil
- ½ teaspoon finely crushed dried jasmine petals

Like wildflowers you must allow yourself to grow in all the places people thought you never would.
– Lorde

Honeysuckle Bath

Makes approximately 1 ½ cups

An uplifting, happiness-inducing bath salt blend that will also soften the skin. This mixture will create enough for one bath. Pour the mixture into a running bath. Lie back and relax for at least 20 minutes. You may like to rinse quickly afterwards but it is not necessary.

You will need

- 1 cup of Himalayan salt
- ¼ cup of bicarbonate of soda
- 1 teaspoon of dried Honeysuckle flowers (*Lonicera spp.*)
- 2 tablespoons Lavender flowers (*Lavandula spp.*)

- 4 tablespoons of dried Rose petals (*Rosa spp.*)
- 5 drops of Bergamot (*Citrus bergamia*) essential oil
- 5 drops of Lavender (*Lavandula spp.*) essential oil
- a glass mixing bowl
- a wooden spoon

To make

Mix together the Himalayan salt and the bicarbonate of soda in the glass bowl. Add the Honeysuckle and Lavender flowers, the Rose petals and the essential oils and mix well. If you wish to create this for a gift or to store, pack it into a sterilised jar and seal. Use within six months.

Daisies are like sunshine to the ground.
– Drew Barrymore

Daisy Faery Feet Soak Spell

Makes approximately 1 cup

A refreshing floral foot soak for those who have been standing for long hours and are suffering from sore, aching feet. The inclusion of energising essential oils and Daisies will lift the spirits as well.

You will need

- ½ cup Himalayan salt
- ½ cup Epsom salts
- 3 drops Peppermint essential oil
- 3 drops Eucalyptus essential oil
- a small handful of dried English Daisies (*Bellis perennis*)
- a large glass bowl
- a wooden spoon
- sterilised glass jar/s

To make

Mix together the salts and essential oils in the large glass bowl with the wooden spoon. Sprinkle the Daisies in with the salts, mix through. Pack into glass jar/s and seal tightly. Store in a cool, dry place. To use, add three heaped tablespoons to a warm foot bath. You may like to add a few fresh Daisies as well.

To make a perfume, take some rose water and wash your hands in it, then take a lavender flower and rub it with your palms, and you will achieve the desired effect.
–Leonardo da Vinci

Lavender Deodorant

Makes 3 tablespoons

A subtle flower-fragranced and completely natural deodorant. Spread a pea-sized amount under each arm.

You will need

- ½ tablespoon vegetable wax
- 3 tablespoons coconut oil
- 1 tablespoon arrowroot powder
- 1 tablespoon bicarbonate of soda
- 6 drops lavender essential oil
- a double boiler or two saucepans you can nest
- whisk
- sterilised container/s

To make

Place the vegetable wax and the coconut oil into the double boiler over a low heat and gently stir to melt. Remove from the heat. Add the arrowroot powder, bicarbonate of soda and the lavender essential oil and whisk until the mixture thickens. Fill sterilised container/s and set aside to cool completely. Don't seal with lids until completely set. Use within 2 months.

Wildflowers can't be controlled, and neither
can the girl with a soul boundless as the sky, and
a spirit as free and wild as the ocean.
– Melody Lee

Calendula Faery Hair Repair Spell

Makes approximately 3 cups

Wash your bad hair days away with this gorgeous nourishing shampoo. This mixture will cleanse, repair and protect your hair. To use, shake well and use as you would your regular shampoo.

You will need

- ½ cup of dried Calendula flowers (*Calendula officinalis*)
- 2 cups of boiling distilled water
- ¼ cup of liquid Castile (vegetable based) soap
- 4 drops of Thyme (*Thymus vulgaris*) essential oil
- 4 drops of Rosemary (*Rosmarinus officinalis*) essential oil
- 4 drops of Rose (*Rosa spp.*) essential oil
- a large heat-proof glass or ceramic bowl
- a wooden spoon
- sterilised bottle/s

To make

Put the Calendula flowers into the large bowl and then pour in the boiling water. Leave for at least 30 minutes or until completely cool. Add the Castile soap and the essential oils. Stir well. Strain then pour into the glass bottle. Keep out of direct sunlight and use within six weeks.

The Gift of Sharing Flowers

More than anything, I must have flowers,
always, and always.
– Claude Monet

For those not immersed in flowers daily, it is perhaps a daunting task to select from the bountiful, bursting display that is the visual and emotional rainbow of most flower-selling places. For us to decide on whether a flower-based perfume, botanical cosmetic or floral décor treasure would be just as inspiring to the recipient as it is for us is probably even more difficult. Usually we gravitate towards what we like, and choose the flower, the fragrance or the bouquet that we like best, all the

while hoping that the recipient will feel equally enchanted by the selection.

In the final section of this book, Flower Lore, I have included useful lists that could help you select flowers that match birthdates, zodiac signs, even days of the week that may align with the person you are gifting flowers to. I've also included The Language of Flowers in a dictionary format for you to explore meanings and the flowers attached to them, so you can send sentiments that say exactly how you feel, or perhaps you could discover flowers that match attitudes and characteristics of your friend or family member by using these floral lists.

This information can help to fill your days with more meaningful flowers and also to create divine nature-inspired and infused treasures for family and friends. Following is a bunch of helpful flower care advice, along with my very favourite recipes for beautiful botanical-infused treasures that I hope will make living with flowers a delight.

I'd rather have roses on my table than
diamonds on my neck.
– Emma Goldman

How to Purchase the Best Fresh Flowers

There are many different places to purchase your flowers from, and each has their own aspects and elements that can help - and sometimes hinder - your quest for floral perfection. Where you purchase your flowers will make a difference in quality, range and how long your flowers will last.

Florists Good florists will not only have quality, well cared-for stock, they will also be happy to give personal assistance in selecting flowers to perfectly suit your needs and provide you with appropriate advice to ensure your flowers look their best and last as long as possible.

Stock will be what is in season and available locally and also imported flowers. As well as bunches of single flower types that

have been cleaned and conditioned, you can purchase styled bouquets and floral designs that are ready to go. Orders can be made of personalised creations that can sometimes be made up for you on the spot or picked up or delivered at an arranged time. Florists can create floral designs for events, special occasions and corporate use. Building a relationship with your local florist not only supports valuable small local business, it can benefit you in having a ready friend in the flower world to help source the blossoms you desire year-round.

Online There are many online services that offer floral delivery, and most work by taking your order from a selection of designs that you can choose from that are displayed online. This order is then given to a florist close to the delivery address. Additional items can be included with your arrangement, such as balloons, wine and champagne, fruit, chocolates, stuffed toys and even hampers, which may be handy for gift-giving. It should be noted that all this can be organised by your local storefront Florist as well and that your local florist, or one close to your gift destination, may also offer direct online ordering and even more personalised floral selection and design. Online floral ordering is very convenient, fast and a good solution for sending distant floral gifts.

Floral Studios These are not places where you can usually walk in and purchase a bunch of flowers, but rather studios to meet with floral designers who specialise in events and corporate work, along with a more tailored floral service. There may be restricted hours or visits are by appointment only. Floral studios sometimes specialise or are known for certain themes or looks, much like fine artists and designers.

Grocery Stores and Supermarkets Flowers are usually conditioned and are sold in single-type bunches, mixed bouquets and sometimes in floral designs in base mediums and display boxes and vases. Flowers are usually cheaper and the turnover can be high, so sometimes flowers are fresh. The problem with flowers from these places is that they are often kept next to the fruit and vegetables where ethylene gas, which is released

naturally from the produce, will speed the decay process of the flowers. Flowers are also often displayed outside and subjected to harsh conditions. That said, sometimes the local grocer has a passion for flowers and a deeper understanding of flower care and takes these points into consideration.

Flower Markets and Wholesalers Most capital cities have a flower market that services the floral industry. Here you can purchase flowers and foliage and sometimes sundry items, such as vases, floristry supplies and display items, at wholesale prices. Not all flower markets and wholesalers are open to the public; for some you will require a business in order to visit/purchase. At a flower market, you will be able to purchase flowers from growers and wholesalers that are grown locally, as well as imported from all over the world.

Farmers and Local Markets You will find cut flower growers, along with florists and flower sellers, at farmers' markets and local markets. Engage the stallholders to find out more about their supply and what you might expect in coming months.

Flower type and quality will vary greatly, depending on the type of stallholder. Farmers will have what is in season and so their range may be limited, but the stock is usually the freshest and so it lasts the longest. Florists at markets will work similarly to those with storefronts, but in the bustling market environment their time for more personal attention may be limited. Their display will include floral designs and styled bouquets and flowers that will be conditioned, but may also include some that are not. Flower sellers purchase elsewhere, like florists do, but usually do not have conditioned and styled flowers and their flowers are less expensive.

Conditioning

This is a term that refers to the care that is given to fresh flowers to ensure they last for as long as possible and are presented in the best possible way. Flowers are conditioned by florists before sale and before they are used in arrangements and designs. Excess foliage and that which will fall below the waterline in vases and

holding buckets is removed; stems are recut, usually at an angle to facilitate good uptake of water; sometimes floral preservatives, biocides and foods are used; flowers are stored in temperatures that are suitable for their type.

When you have only two pennies left in the world, buy a loaf of bread with one, and a lily with the other.
– Chinese Proverb

What to Look for When Buying Flowers

It is rather disheartening to buy what seems like a gorgeous fresh bunch of flowers and wake up the next day to a wilted, sad mess in a vase. Let's explore what you need to look for when selecting your flowers. Overall, beware of pests, diseases, physical damage, blackening and wilting.

Position Make sure that the flowers are not standing in full sun, directly under heating or air-conditioning or in front of fans, as all of these will dry out and shorten your flowers' lifespan. Flowers should also not be overcrowded, as this leads to fungal issues. They must not be displayed with fruit and vegetables as the ethylene gas emitted from produce will drastically reduce the life of the flowers.

Water Gently move the flowers if they are in buckets or observe vases and look at the water they are standing in. It should be ample and look fresh and clear. Any sign of a decaying smell, slime or mould should be your sign to pass those flowers over.

Flowers Overall, look for a fresh and firm appearance with even colour on each flower. Flowers that have pollen present mean that they are at the end of their vase life. Ensure that the blooms are not damaged by overcrowding, as sometimes it can be hard to see the condition of flowers that are tightly displayed. Overcrowding also leads to poor air circulation, which encourages bacterial growth and leads to a drastically shortened vase life. Although you may think that the odd wilted flower is okay, it is emitting the dreaded ethylene and this will reduce the

life of the rest of the flowers, so look for bunches without dying or dead blossoms. Fully opened flowers are also at the end of their life, so perhaps look for flowers that have half-opened buds. Not all flowers will continue to open once they are cut and this includes some roses and dahlias.

Stems These should be even in length, straight, firm to the touch and free from damage. Look out for torn ends because these will impede water uptake, as will uneven stem length. The overall stem should be firm and of a fresh appearance without discolouration, mould or slime. Make sure that the stems are not split.

Foliage Leaves must be of a healthy, fresh appearance. Note any discoloration, mould, slime or damage. Foliage should not be below the water when purchasing conditioned flowers in arrangements ready for display.

Ethylene Gas

Most flowers are sensitive to ethylene which is emitted from decaying plant material (from other flowers and foliage), ripening fruit, cigarette smoke and engine fumes. Exposure leads to drastically reduced vase life, so effort should be made to avoid it by removing dying flowers and foliage in displays and ensuring thoughtful positioning away from ethylene sources.

Flower First Aid

Here are a few ways to save wilting flowers. They will not work all of the time as flowers do have a lifespan and perhaps yours are at an end, but it's worth trying some of these tips to revive flowers that may be subjected to blockages and inhospitable climates.

Recutting stems will help remove air embolisms, blockage or decay in the stem. Try recutting the stem at an angle, above any discolouration you can see. You can also snip up the stem vertically about 1–2.5 cm/1 inch, as this increases the surface area for water uptake. After recutting, place swiftly place in fresh warm water.

Plunging in boiling water is not suitable for all flowers but for those with stronger, especially woody stems, it will help to

quickly revive them. Roses benefit immensely from this method. Protect the flower heads by wrapping in paper and holding firmly to avoid steaming them. Pour about a cup of boiling water into a heat-proof vessel. You only want about 1–2 cm/½ to 1 inch of water. The harder the stem, the longer you can stand in the water. For example: Roses need about 30 seconds. The heat helps the water to rise quickly and effectively make its way to the flower.

Soaking flowers in a bath of room temperature water is an effective way to help revive Orchids and most tropical flowers.

Misting is another favourite of tropical flowers and is also a good way to revive Boronias and Violets.

Wrapping and soaking can assist Roses, Sunflowers and many other flowers that have wilted. First lay out your flowers on a sheet of paper and gently straighten their heads. Wrap tightly so that flower heads at straight within the paper and seal with tape. Stand in a vase containing conditioning solution for 4 to 6 hours and then unwrap.

Flower Food

This flower preservative and food mixture is suitable for most flowers. No need to dilute, simply mix together well and place your flowers into it.

- 2 tablespoons of vinegar
- 2 teaspoon sugar
- 1 teaspoon white vinegar
- ½ teaspoon bleach
- 2 L/4 pt water

I wish I could do whatever I liked behind the curtain of 'madness'. Then: I'd arrange flowers, all day long …
– Frida Kahlo

How to Care for Your Flowers at Home

If your flowers are already conditioned and arranged by a florist, then there should be nothing you need to do other than

place them in water and then ensure they are well hydrated. If not, then follow the first few steps below to get your flowers in top shape for a beautiful and long vase life. You will still need to maintain your flowers, however they come to you, so read through to make sure you have filled up on flower homecare wisdom.

1. Select a suitable container for your flowers. It should support them without letting them become overcrowded, be able to hold enough water, and should never be metal as this is usually toxic to flowers.
2. Remove all the leaves that will be underwater in the container they will be living in.
3. Cut off at least 2 cm from the end of the stems.
4. Decide on usage of a flower food/preservative and add to water if desired. This is not recommended for most Southern Hemisphere native flowers and it can prevent heavily woody stems from taking up water.

5. Position the vase in an area that is free from extreme temperatures, direct sunlight, drafts, air-conditioning, smoke and fruit. Ensure good ventilation.
6. Refresh water every 2 to 3 days.
7. Remove spent and dying flowers and foliage and recut the stems if they are discoloured.

Flowers don't tell, they show.
– Stephanie Skeem

How to Cut Garden Flowers

If you are growing flowers at home, there are better times and ways to harvest them to ensure the best vase life possible.

- Pick flowers in the morning as flower stems are at their most hydrated at that time. Never harvest flowers on very hot days as they will most likely be suffering somewhat from water stress.
- Have a bucket of water with you and place stems into it as

soon as you cut them.

- Pick most flowers when they are just starting to open. Some types may not continue to open though, such as various Roses and Dahlias.
- Gladioli, Foxglove and Snapdragons will continue to open if you pick them when the first flowers are appearing, but
Delphiniums will not, so it is better to wait until all of them have begun to blossom.
- Though 'deadheading' (the removal of spent blossoms) is important, don't overharvest fresh flowers from perennial plants and shrubs as you may find fewer flowers the following season. Most annuals, however, will reward you with constant new flowers over their life if they are picked regularly.

I paint flowers so they will not die.
– Frida Kahlo

Preserving Flowers

No matter how much we love and care for them, flowers have a lifespan. We can preserve them and their beauty by drying and pressing and then use them in art and craft works to give them new lives. There are many ways to achieve this and your selection will depend on whether you want your flowers flat or to keep some of their form and shape.

The time-honoured way to preserve flowers is by pressing them. Botanists and explorers have pressed flowers throughout time to support their record-keeping of the lands they have found, as much as others have wanted to prolong the life of blooms given as a token of love forever. Once pressed, the flowers can be used to create cards, framed floral arrangements, or to decorate candles and other items. They can also be set under glass and within resin to create jewellery and décor items.

Create a Flower Press

These are incredibly easy to make and are the very best way to press flowers, because they are gentle on delicate flowers and pressure can be completely controlled. They also make gorgeous gifts and can be decorated with pressed flowers or floral artwork. The size will be personal, but I would suggest that you do not make a flower press larger than 20 cm x 20 cm/8 in x 8 in in size. Pressure needs to be maintained through the press and the larger it gets, the harder that is to achieve in the centre of the press. Don't use corrugated cardboard in your press, as this can leave unsightly lines across your pressed flowers.

You will need

- 2 pieces of smooth wood
- a newspaper
- blotting paper
- a sheet of heavy craft cardboard/acetate
- scissors

- heavy tape
- drill
- 4 wing nuts
- 8 metal washers
- 4 bolts
- tweezers
- flowers/leaves

To make

Tape the two pieces of wood together. Drill a hole in each corner through both pieces of wood to suit the size of your bolts. Take the tape off and discard. Create a template to cut your paper layers for your press with the heavy cardboard/acetate sheet. Trace around one of the wood pieces and place a dot where each of the drill holes are with a pen. Cut out the shape and snip off each corner and least 1 cm/½ in in from the drill hole mark.

To use

- Have your flowers/leaves ready for pressing. Make sure

they are clean and completely dry. Cut out a stack of newspaper and blotting paper shapes using the template. Begin by laying 2 sheets of newspaper on the bottom of the press, then a sheet of blotting paper. Carefully place the flowers/petals/leaves on the blotting paper, using tweezers if necessary, keeping clear of the edges of the press and not allowing any floral material to overlap. Place another sheet of blotting paper on top followed by two sheets of newspaper and then repeat.

- You can fill the press with between six and 10 layers of flowers/leaves, depending on the thickness of the plant material you are pressing. Thicker materials are better pressed with only a few layers. Place the wooden press top in position and then thread the bolts and washers into place and fasten with wing nuts.
- Tie a tag to one of the bolts that lists the contents and the date. Store in a dry, warm place for six weeks before opening. Once you remove them from the press, store the flowers flat in paper bags until ready for use.

Air Drying Flowers

Another traditional way of preserving flowers is to simply hang them or lay them on racks in a well-ventilated, dark place. Some flowers can also be dried out by standing them in empty vases, such as Agapanthus, Dahlia, Hyacinth, Hydrangea and Sweet Williams, while others will naturally bow their heads so are far better hung. Some flowers that do very well hung are Peony, Rose, Statice, Lavender, Delphinium, Carnation and Jasmine. Leave where they are until ready for use.

Desiccant Preservation

If you wish to dry flowers/foliage and keep their shapes then using a desiccant, such as silica gel crystals, borax, sand or alum, will help you achieve very good results. Flowers may need to be wired before using if they are to be put into arrangements. To use desiccant preservation, airtight plastic containers are best. Ensure whatever you are using as a desiccant is finely crushed. Layer about 2 cm/1 in of desiccant

into the bottom of the container and then place your flowers evenly on it, without overlapping. Gently fill the container with additional desiccant until the flowers are completely covered. Seal and leave for at least two weeks. Check regularly. When flowers are dry, take them out, shake off excess desiccant and then store flowers in cardboard boxes in a cool, dry place until ready for. Dry out the desiccant so it is ready for reuse, by spreading it out over a baking sheet and placing in an oven.

Oven Drying

This method can be achieved through the use of a microwave or traditional oven. It can be very hard to control, with flowers drying out too fast and even burning. Spread flowers, without overlapping, on a baking sheet covered in baking paper and dry out in a slow oven until ready. In the microwave, lay out flowers on baking paper on a microwave-proof plate and cook in short bursts of 10 seconds until dry.

If I had a flower for every time you made me smile and laugh, I'd have a garden to walk in forever.
– Anonymous

Flower Chandelier

This divine floral installation can be hung over a dinner table or in a room to give it instant lush, botanical beauty. You can use a glue gun, but these do burn flowers and leaves, so a speciality florist glue (obtainable from florist and craft suppliers) is a far better choice. You will need to hold each blossom and leaf in place for a few moments, but the results will be beautiful. You may wish to add seasonal or occasion-appropriate decorations, such as bells, stars and so on, or even light your chandelier with a twist of fairy lights!

You will need

- hula hoop
- florist glue or glue gun
- selection of dried or fresh flowers and foliage

- ribbon
- additional decorations (optional)

To make

- Tie four pieces of ribbon, the length that you need to suit the place you are hanging it from, to four equally-spaced points around your hoop. I like to glue these in place for added security.
- Begin with your foliage and create a base for your flowers by gluing to cover entire hoop.
- Next, glue the larger flowers into place as you desire and follow these with filler (smaller blossoms). Finish by tying all ribbons together and make a loop to hang. You can add additional silk flowers and decorations. If adding fairy lights, you may wish to twist these into the design after you complete the foliage layer and before you add the flowers.

No matter how chaotic it is, wildflowers will still spring up in the middle of nowhere.
– Sheryl Crow

Floral Lining Paper

Will create up to 12 standard drawer liners

I adore creating my own traditional lining papers because I find that I can somehow capture the essence of my garden or flowers I've been gifted, and enjoy them every time I open my cupboards and drawers. It is so easy to do - why don't you try it with your favourite blossoms? You can substitute the vanilla essential oil for any skin-safe oil you prefer.

You will need

- wallpaper (ensure it is not pre-pasted)
- a soft cloth
- a small bowl
- 10 drops vanilla oil

- 1 teaspoon sweet almond oil
- 1 cup potpourri
- a large sealable plastic bag

To make

- Measure your shelves or drawer bottoms and cut the wallpaper to size.
- Mix the vanilla oil and the sweet almond oil together in the small bowl. Using the soft cloth, wipe the oil mixture lightly all over the top side of a sheet of cut wallpaper. Sprinkle the potpourri over the top of this. Lay the next sheet of wallpaper on top and repeat oil and potpourri layers. Once complete, roll and place into sealable plastic bag. Store this bag in a warm and dry place for a few weeks. Take out and shake. The liners are ready to use.

Note: the potpourri can be placed in a container and used as a room freshener and the bag can be reused to carry clothing items when travelling.

The Gift of
Flower Lore

Flowers reflect the human search for meaning. Does not each of us, no matter how our life has gone, ache to have a life as beautiful and true to itself as that of a flower?
– Phillip Moffitt

Have you ever looked at a flower and wondered what it meant, why you were attracted to it or what divine gifts or messages it may hold for you? Understanding the meanings of flowers and the special correspondences each flower has with days of the week, months, gods, goddesses, places and times can enhance the way you interact, use and align with flowers, making for more personal arrangements, gifts and floral creativity.

The Language of Flowers

A

Absence: Zinnia (*Zinnia elegans*)

Ability to be happy: Iris, Blue Flag (*Iris versicolor*)

Abuse, do not: Safflower (*Carthamus tinctorius*)

Abundance: Carnation (*Dianthus caryophyllus*), Jasmine (*Jasminum officinale*), Peruvian Lily (*Alstroemeria spp.*), Roman Chamomile (*Chamaemelum nobile*), Stargazer Lily, Pink (*Lilium orientalis*), Marsh Marigold (*Caltha palustris*), Honesty (*Lunaria annua*)

Acceptance: Magnolia (*Magnolia campbellii*), Scottish Primrose (*Primula scotica*)

Achievement: Rose, Mlle Cécile Brünner (*Rosa* 'Cécile Brünner')

Acknowledgment: Canterbury Bells (*Campanula medium*)

Action, positive: Scotch Thistle (*Onopordum acanthium*)

Acquaintance: Pelargonium (*Pelargonium cucullatum*)

Adaptability: Rose, Cherokee (*Rosa laevigata*)

Admiration: Lavender (*Lavandula stoechas*), Heather, Lavender (*Calluna vulgaris*), Purple Orchid (*Cattleya skinneri*)

Admire you, I: Heather, Lavender (*Calluna vulgaris*)

Adorable, you are: Camellia, White (*Camellia*)

Adoration: Heliconia (*Heliconia spp.*)

Adversity, patience in: Chamomile, German (*Matricaria chamomilla*)

Affection: Thyme (*Thymus vulgaris*), Stock (*Matthiola incana*), Celosia (*Celosia spp.*), Crown Vetch (*Securigera varia*), Morning Glory (*Ipomoea purpurea*), Kalanchoe (*Kalanchoe spp.*), Carnation, White (*Dianthus caryophyllus*)

Afterthought: Aster (*Aster spp.*), Michaelmas Daisy (*Aster amellus*)

Again, begin: Rose, Miniature (*Rosa spp.*)

Agreement: Rose, dark pink (*Rosa spp.*), Phlox (*Phlox spp.*)

Alchemy: Honesty (*Lunaria annua*), Hellebore (*Helleborus spp.*)

Alert, be: Sundew (*Drosera auriculata*)

Alignment, chakras: Lilac (*Syringa vulgaris*)

Alignment, female: Easter Lily (*Lilium longiflorum*)

Altruism: Peach Blossom (*Prunus persica*)

Alleviate: Lovage (*Levisticum officinale*)

Ambassador of love: Rose, Cabbage (*Rosa × centifolia*)

Ambition: Hollyhock (*Alcea rosea*), Stargazer Lily, Pink (*Lilium orientalis*), Pomegranate Blossom (*Punica granatum*)

Ambition, female: Hollyhock, White (*Alcea rosea*)

Ambition, modest: Trillium (*Trillium spp.*)

Amiability: Fuchsia (*Fuchsia magellanica*)

Animosity: St John's Wort (*Hypericum perforatum*)

Anger: Petunia (*Petunia spp.*)

Anger dissipated: Althea (*Hibiscus syriacus*)

Anger, release: Burdock (*Arctium spp.*)

Anniversary, happy: Tree Peony (*Paeonia suffruticosa*)

Answers: Cooktown Orchid (*Vappodes phalaenopsis*), Rafflesia (*Rafflesia arnoldii*), Violet, Blue (*Viola sororia*)

Anxiety: Scottish Primrose (*Primula scotica*), Columbine (*Aquilegia vulgaris*), American Pasqueflower (*Pulsatilla hirsutissima*)

Anything is possible: Delphinium (*Delphinium spp.*)

Apology: Flannel Flower (*Actinotus helianthi*)

Appreciate you, I: Gerbera Daisy (*Gerbera jamesonii*), Lisianthus (*Eustoma grandiflorum*), Rose, peach (*Rosa spp.*)

Appreciation: Poinsettia (*Euphorbia pulcherrima*), Gerbera Daisy (*Gerbera jamesonii*), Lisianthus (*Eustoma grandiflorum*), Rose, dark pink (*Rosa spp.*)

Ardent love: Carnation, White (*Dianthus caryophyllus*)

Arguments, end: Honeysuckle (*Lonicera spp.*)

Articulation: Celandine (*Ficaria verna*)

Assertiveness: Geraldton Wax (*Chamelaucium uncinatum*), Sunflower (*Helianthus annuus*)

Attainment: Tea Tree (*Leptospermum myrsinoides*)

Attention seeking: Heliconia (*Heliconia spp.*)

Attitude: Cooktown Orchid (*Vappodes phalaenopsis*), Red Hot Poker (*Kniphofia spp.*)

Attract love: Lady's Mantle (*Alchemilla vulgaris*), Lovage (*Levisticum officinale*), Chamomile, German (*Matricaria chamomilla*)

Attract wealth: Chamomile, Roman (*Chamaemelum nobile*)

Attraction: Moon Orchid (*Amabilis Phalaenopsis*)

Attraction, beauty is your only: Rose, Beach (*Rosa rugosa*)

Attractiveness: Ranunculus (*Ranunculus spp.*)

Austerity: Thistle, Common (*Cirsium vulgare*), Sea Holly (*Eryngium maritimum*)

Awaken: American Pasqueflower (*Pulsatilla hirsutissima*)

Awareness: Gardenia (*Gardenia jasminoides*), Queen Anne's Lace (*Daucus carota*), Bells of Ireland (*Moluccella laevis*), Rose, Prairie (*Rosa arkansana*)

Awareness, sensory: Texas Bluebonnet (*Lupinus texensis*)

B

Balance: Bottlebrush (*Callistemon linearis*), Hawthorn (*Crataegus monogyna*), Meadowsweet (*Filipendula ulmaria*), Vanilla (*Vanilla planifolia*)

Balance emotions: Lemon Balm (*Melissa officinalis*), Prairie Crocus (*Pulsatilla patens*)

Balance, female: Evening Primrose (*Oenothera*)

Balance, spiritual: Passion Flower (*Passiflora incarnata*)

Balanced energy: Pasqueflower (*Pulsatilla vulgaris*)

Banish negative thoughts: Lemon (*Citrus limon*)

Banishing: Hellebore (*Helleborus*), Yarrow (*Achillea millefolium*)

Barriers, release: Lady's Mantle (*Alchemilla vulgaris*)

Bashful love: Rose, Deep Red (*Rosa*)

Bashfulness: Blushing Bride (*Tillandsia ionantha*), Primrose (*Primula vulgaris*)

Be alert: Sundew (*Drosera auriculata*)

Be brave: Waratah (*Telopea speciosissima*), Heather, White (*Calluna vulgaris*)

Be happy: Shasta Daisy (*Leucanthemum maximum*), Lily of the Valley (*Convallaria majalis*), Honeysuckle (*Lonicera*)

Be mine: Carnation, Red (*Dianthus caryophyllus*)

Be present in this moment: Baby's Breath (*Gypsophila paniculata*)

Be quiet: Belladonna (*Atropa belladonna*)

Be still: Belladonna (*Atropa belladonna*), Aconite (*Aconite*)

Be strong: Sunflower (*Helianthus annuus*)

Be true to yourself: Aster (*Aster*)

Be with you, I want to: Rose, Dark Pink (*Rosa*), Petunia (*Petunia*)

Beauty: Rose, Red (*Rosa*), Heather, Lavender (*Calluna vulgaris*),

Cosmos (*Cosmos*), Frangipani (*Plumeria alba*), Sweet Pea (*Lathyrus odoratus*), Heather, Lavender (*Calluna vulgaris*), Apricot (*Prunus armeniaca*)

Beginning: Mulla Mulla (*Ptilotus exaltatus*), Snowdrop (*Galanthus nivalis*), Rose, Yellow (*Rosa*), Jade (*Crassula ovata*), Bloodroot (*Sanguinaria canadensis*), Rose, Miniature (*Rosa*)

Belief: Passion Flower (*Passiflora incarnata*), Iris, Fairy (*Dietes grandiflora*), Tulip, Red (*Tulipa*), Foxglove (*Digitalis purpurea*), Iris, Blue Flag (*Iris versicolor*)

Belonging: Hibiscus, White (*Hibiscus arnottianus*), Primrose (*Primula vulgaris*)

Betrayal: Rose, Wild (*Rosa acicularis*), Iris, Fairy (*Dietes grandiflora*)

Beware: Foxglove (*Digitalis purpurea*), Heath, Bell (*Erica cinerea*), Rhododendron (*Rhododendron spp.*)

Birth: Tree Peony (*Paeonia suffruticosa*)

Blocks, release: Iris, Blue Flag (*Iris versicolor*), Lime (*Tilia x*

europaea), Star of Bethlehem (*Ornithogalum spp.*)

Bluntness: Borage (*Borago officinalis*)

Boundaries: Rose, Mlle Cécile Brünner (*Rosa* 'Cécile Brünner'), Chrysanthemum, Yellow (*Chrysanthemum spp.*), Gladiola (*Gladiolus spp.*)

Bravery: Heather, White (*Calluna vulgaris*), Waratah (*Telopea speciosissima*), Edelweiss (*Leontopodium alpinum*)

Breathe: Baby's Breath (*Gypsophila paniculata*), Crocus (*Crocus*)

Brotherly love: Lilac (*Syringa vulgaris*)

C

Calculated risks: Oleander (*Nerium oleander*)

Calm: Flannel Flower (*Actinotus helianthi*), Daisy (*Bellis perennis*), Camellia, Japanese (*Camellia japonica*), Geranium, Rose (*Pelargonium graveolens*), Evening Primrose (*Oenothera*), Chamomile, Roman (*Chamaemelum nobile*), Statice (*Limonium*), Lemon Balm (*Melissa officinalis*),

Sweet Marjoram (*Origanum marjorana*), Tiger Lily (*Lilium tigrinum*), Lily of the Valley (*Convallaria majalis*), Lisianthus (*Eustoma grandiflorum*), Pasqueflower (*Pulsatilla vulgaris*), Speedwell (*Veronica officinalis*)

Caution: Oleander (*Nerium oleander*)

Celebration: Gerbera Daisy (*Gerbera jamesonii*)

Chakra alignment: Lilac (*Syringa vulgaris*)

Challenge: Violet Nightshade (*Solanum brownii*), Cayenne (*Capsicum frutescens*), Nasturtium (*Tropaeolum majus*)

Chance, second: Sacred Blue Lily (*Nymphaea caerulea*)

Change: Bee Balm (*Monarda spp.*), Scarlet Pimpernel (*Anagallis arvensis*), Mayflower (*Epigaea repens*), Crowfoot (*Erodium crinitum*), Magnolia (*Magnolia campbellii*)

Charm: Ranunculus (*Ranunculus*), Cowslip (*Primula veris*)

Charisma: Moon Orchid (*Amabilis Phalaenopsis*)

Chastity: Lily of the Valley (*Convallaria majalis*)

Cheerfulness: Buttercup (*Ranunculus acris*), Chrysanthemum, Florist's (*Chrysanthemum morifolium*), Shasta Daisy (*Leucanthemum maximum*), Gerbera Daisy (*Gerbera jamesonii*), Crocus (*Crocus*), Hibiscus, Native Yellow (*Hibiscus brackenridgei*)

Choices, positive: African Daisy (*Osteospermum*), Lily of the Valley (*Convallaria majalis*)

Clarity: Boronia (*Boronia ledifolia*), Sweet Alyssum (*Alyssum maritimum*), Angel's Trumpet (*Brugmansia candida*), Dandelion (*Taraxacum officinale*), Love-in-a-Mist (*Nigella damascena*), Gerbera Daisy, Yellow (*Gerbera jamesonii*)

Cleansing: Bottlebrush (*Callistemon linearis*), Lavender (*Lavandula stoechas*), Calendula (*Calendula officinalis*), Primrose (*Primula vulgaris*), Lemon Blossom (*Citrus limon*)

Clearing, space: Lilac (*Syringa vulgaris*)

Come back: Rose, Yellow (*Rosa spp.*)

Come home: Native Geranium (*Geranium solanderi*)

Comfort: Sweet Pea (*Lathyrus odoratus*), Lisianthus (*Eustoma grandiflorum*), Geranium, Rose (*Pelargonium graveolens*), Heartsease (*Viola tricolor*)

Commitment: Wedding Bush (*Ricinocarpos pinifolius*), Ranunculus (*Ranunculus*)

Communication: Delphinium (*Delphinium*), Stephanotis (*Stephanotis floribunda*)

Compassion: Carnation, Red (*Dianthus caryophyllus*), Peony (*Paeonia officinalis*), Rose, Musk (*Rosa moschata*), Bleeding Heart (*Lamprocapnos spectabilis*), Bee Balm (*Monarda*), Heartsease (*Viola tricolor*), Basil (*Ocimum basilicum*), Scottish Primrose (*Primula scotica*)

Competition, healthy: Tiger Lily (*Lilium tigrinum*)

Concentration: Clematis (*Clematis*), Camellia, Japanese (Camellia japonica)

Confidence: Frangipani (*Plumeria alba*), Poet's Narcissus (*Narcissus poeticus*), Sunflower (*Helianthus annuus*), Dahlia

(*Dahlia*), Lilac (*Syringa vulgaris*), Heather, White (*Calluna vulgaris*), Foxglove (*Digitalis purpurea*)

Congratulations: Sundew (*Drosera auriculata*), Tea Tree (*Leptospermum myrsinoides*), Jasmine (*Jasminum officinale*), Amaryllis (*Amaryllis spp.*), Bouvardia (*Bouvardia spp.*)

Consciousness: Rafflesia (*Rafflesia arnoldii*), Sacred Blue Lily (*Nymphaea caerulea*), Passion Flower (*Passiflora incarnata*)

Consideration: Hibiscus, White (*Hibiscus arnottianus*)

Courage: Waratah (*Telopea speciosissima*), King Protea (*Protea cynaroides*), Rose, Red (*Rosa*), Heather, White (*Calluna vulgaris*), Primrose (*Primula vulgaris*), Garlic (*Allium sativum*), Mullein (*Verbascum Thapsus*), Borage (*Borago officinalis*), Thistle, Common (*Cirsium vulgare*)

Creativity: Grevillea (*Grevillea banksii*), Honey Grevillea (*Grevillea eriostachya*), King Protea (*Protea cynaroides*), Siberian Iris (*Iris sibirica*), Dahlia (*Dahlia*), Foxglove (*Digitalis purpurea*), Iris, Blue Flag Marigold (*Tagetes erecta*)

D

Danger: Rhododendron (*Rhododendron*)

Death: Yew (*Taxus baccata*), California Poppy (*Eschscholzia californica*), Jonquil (*Narcissus jonquilla*), Red Hot Poker (*Kniphofia*), Blackberry (*Rubus fruticosus*)

Deceit: Mock Orange (*Philadelphus*), Venus Flytrap (*Dionaea muscipula*), Dogbane (*Apocynum cannabinum*)

Declaration of love: Red Tulip (*Tulipa*)

Declaration of war: Tansy (*Tanacetum vulgare*)

Dedication: Wedding Bush (*Ricinocarpos pinifolius*), Edelweiss (*Leontopodium alpinum*)

Defence: Mayflower (*Epigaea repens*), Patchouli (*Pogostemon cablin*)

Desire: Red Tulip (*Tulipa*), Althea (*Hibiscus syriacus*), Tulip, Wild (*Tulipa sprengeri*), Jonquil (*Narcissus jonquilla*), Hibiscus, Red (*Hibiscus rosa-sinensis*)

Detachment: Sacred Lotus (*Nelumbo nucifera*), Bleeding Heart (*Lamprocapnos spectabilis*)

Determination: Amaryllis (*Amaryllis*), Ginger (*Zingiber officinale*)

Devotion: Peruvian Lily (*Alstroemeria*), Heliotrope (Heliotropium), Carnation, White (*Dianthus caryophyllus*)

Difference, respect for: Stephanotis (*Stephanotis floribunda*)

Dignity: Calla Lily (*Zantedeschia aethiopica*), Dahlia (*Dahlia*), Echinacea (*Echinacea purpurea*)

Direction: Pink Heath (*Epacris impressa*)

Direction, new: Edelweiss (*Leontopodium alpinum*)

Dislike: Lobelia, Blue (*Lobelia*)

Do not forget me: Speedwell (*Veronica officinalis*)

Do not give up hope: Petunia (*Petunia spp.*)

Do not touch me: Burdock (*Arctium spp.*)

Do not despair: Chamomile, Roman (*Chamaemelum nobile*)

Dreams: Queen of the Night (*Selenicereus grandiflorus*) California Poppy (*Eschscholzia californica*), Monkshood (Aconitum)

E

Eagerness: Pelargonium (*Pelargonium cucullatum*)

Ego: Gladiola (*Gladiolus*), Witch hazel (*Hamamelis virginiana*)

Elegance: Yarrow (*Achillea millefolium*), Geranium (*Geranium*), Aster (*Aster*)

Emotional blocks, release: Lime (*Tilia x europaea*)

Emotional breakthrough/s: Belladonna (*Atropa belladonna*)

Emotional clarity: Love-in-a-Mist (*Nigella damascena*), Gerbera Daisy, Yellow (*Gerbera jamesonii*)

Emotional development: Gerbera Daisy, White (*Gerbera jamesonii*)

Emotional strength: Gerbera Daisy, Red (*Gerbera jamesonii*)

Emotional warmth: Evening Primrose (*Oenothera spp.*)

Empowerment: Hibiscus, Native Yellow (*Hibiscus brackenridgei*)

Encouragement: Madonna Lily (*Lilium candidum*), Carnation, Pink (*Dianthus caryophyllus*), Dahlia (*Dahlia spp.*), Black-Eyed Susan (*Rudbeckia hirta*)

End arguments: Honeysuckle (*Lonicera spp.*)

Endurance: Everlasting Daisy (*Rhodanthe chlorocephala*), Kalanchoe (*Kalanchoe*), Wisteria (*Wisteria sinensis*)

Enduring love: Wisteria (*Wisteria sinensis*)

Energy: Swamp Lily (*Crinum pedunculatum*), Forsythia (*Forsythia*), Chamomile, German (*Matricaria chamomilla*)

Enlightenment: Water Lily (*Nymphaea spp.*), Hibiscus, White (*Hibiscus rosa-sinensis*)

Enthusiasm: Orange Banksia (*Banksia ashbyi*), Rose, orange (*Rosa*), Orange Blossom (*Citrus x sinensis*), Petunia (*Petunia*), Morning Glory (*Ipomoea purpurea*), Dog Rose (*Rosa canina*), Gayfeather (*Liatris*), Old Man Banksia (*Banksia serrata*)

Error: Bee Orchid (*Ophrys apifera*), Fly Orchid (*Ophrys insectifera*)

Eternal love: Orange Blossom (*Citrus x sinensis*), Heliotrope (*Heliotropium*), Mexican Orange Blossom (*Choisya ternata*)

Everlasting love: Baby's Breath (*Gypsophila paniculata*), Ranunculus (*Ranunculus spp.*)

Evil, protection from: Meadowsweet (*Filipendula ulmaria*), Cranes bill (*Geranium maculatum*), Elder (*Sambucus nigra*), Vervain (*Verbena officinalis*)

Excellence: Camellia, Japanese (*Camellia japonica*), Bird of Paradise (*Strelitzia reginae*), Calendula (*Calendula officinalis*)

Expanded horizons: Stargazer Lily, Pink (*Lilium orientalis*), Purslane (*Portulaca oleracea*)

F

Failure to change: Siberian Iris (*Iris sibirica*)

Faith: Dahlia (*Dahlia*), Gladiola (*Gladiolus*), Heather, White (*Calluna vulgaris*), Canterbury Bells (*Campanula medium*), Columbine (*Aquilegia vulgaris*), Iris, Blue Flag (*Iris versicolor*),

Marguerite Daisy (*Argyranthemum frutescens*), Iris, German (*Iris germanica*)

Farewell: Michaelmas Daisy (*Aster amellus*)

Fascination: Rose, orange (*Rosa*), Honesty (*Lunaria annua*)

Feel, I want to tell you how I: Bleeding Heart (*Lamprocapnos spectabilis*)

Feelings for you, I have new: Delphinium (*Delphinium*)

Feelings, true: Fuchsia (*Fuchsia magellanica*), Poinsettia (*Euphorbia pulcherrima*)

Female energies: Magnolia (*Magnolia campbellii*), Queen Anne's Lace (*Daucus carota*)

Fertility: Lily (*Lilium*), St John's Wort (*Hypericum perforatum*), Orange Blossom (*Citrus x sinensis*), Wisteria (*Wisteria sinensis*), Opium Poppy (*Papaver somniferum*), Geranium (*Geranium*), Patchouli (*Pogostemon cablin*)

Fidelity: Wallflower (*Erysimum*), Speedwell (*Veronica officinalis*)

First love: Dog Violet (*Viola riviniana*), Primrose (*Primula vulgaris*), Periwinkle (*Vinca minor*)

Flexibility: Feverfew (*Tanacetum parthenium*)

Focus: Pink Heath (*Epacris impressa*), Sundew (*Drosera auriculata*), Stock (*Matthiola incana*)

Folly: Columbine (*Aquilegia vulgaris*), Geranium, Scarlet (*Pelargonium*)

Forget you, I will never: Pussytoes (*Antennaria*), Carnation, Pink (*Dianthus caryophyllus*)

Forgiveness: White Tulip (*Tulipa*), Kangaroo Paw (*Anigozanthos manglesii*), Calla Lily (*Zantedeschia aethiopica*), Scottish Primrose (*Primula scotica*), Texas Bluebonnet (*Lupinus texensis*)

Fortitude: Everlasting Daisy (*Rhodanthe chlorocephala*), Chamomile (*Chamaemelum nobile*), Elder (*Sambucus nigra*)

Fortune, good: Goldenrod (*Solidago virgaurea*), Red Clover (*Trifolium pratense*), Apricot (*Prunus armeniaca*)

Freedom: Water Ribbons (*Triglochin procerum*), Frangipani (*Plumeria alba*)

Freedom, creative: Nasturtium (*Tropaeolum majus*)

Friendship: Yarrow (*Achillea millefolium*), Peruvian Lily (*Alstroemeria*), Shasta Daisy (*Leucanthemum maximum*), Freesia (*Freesia*), Rose, Yellow (*Rosa*), Kalanchoe (*Kalanchoe*), Yellow Jessamine (*Gelsemium sempervirens*), Chrysanthemum, Bronze (*Chrysanthemum*), Melissa (*Melissa officinalis*), Mullein, White (*Verbascum Thapsus*), Passionfruit (*Passiflora edulis*), Phlox, Pink (*Phlox*), Rose, Pink (*Rosa*)

G

Generosity: Royal Bluebell (*Wahlenbergia gloriosa*), Tree Peony (*Paeonia suffruticosa*), Dahlia (*Dahlia*)

Gentleness: Mock Orange (*Philadelphus*), Primrose (*Primula vulgaris*), Marguerite Daisy (*Argyranthemum frutescens*), Lewis Mock Orange (*Philadelphus lewisii*)

Get well: Blue Gum Flower (*Eucalyptus globulus*), Native Geranium (*Geranium solanderi*), Swamp Lily (*Crinum pedunculatum*), Sunflower (*Helianthus annuus*), Rose, pale pink (*Rosa*)

Good health: Tree Peony (*Paeonia suffruticosa*), Peony (*Paeonia officinalis*)

Good luck: Tea Tree (*Leptospermum myrsinoides*), Sweet Pea (*Lathyrus odoratus*), Tree Peony (*Paeonia suffruticosa*), Carnation Pink (*Dianthus caryophyllus*), Stephanotis (*Stephanotis floribunda*), Heather, Lavender (*Calluna vulgaris*), Bells of Ireland (*Moluccella laevis*)

Gratitude: Sweet Pea (*Lathyrus odoratus*), Bluebell, Common (*Hyacinthoides non-scripta*), Carnation, Pink (*Dianthus caryophyllus*), Lisianthus (*Eustoma grandiflorum*), Rose, Dark Pink (*Rosa*), Calendula (*Calendula officinalis*), Canterbury Bells (*Campanula medium*)

Grace: Lavender (*Lavandula stoechas*), Orchid (*Orchidaceae*), Rose, pale pink (*Rosa*), Snapdragon (*Antirrhinum majus*), Water Lily, Pink (*Nymphaea*)

Grief: Sturt's Desert Pea (*Swainsona formosa*), Calendula (*Calendula officinalis*)

Grounding: Native Geranium (*Geranium solanderi*), Marsh Marigold (*Caltha palustris*)

Growth: Rose, Prairie (*Rosa arkansana*), Water Hyacinth (*Eichbornia crassipes*), Sacred Lotus (*Nelumbo nucifera*), Angel's Trumpet (*Brugmansia candida*)

Guidance: Bee Balm (*Monarda*), Gardenia (*Gardenia jasminoides*), Freesia (*Freesia*)

H

Happiness: Daisy (*Bellis perennis*), Sunflower (*Helianthus annuus*), Shasta Daisy (*Leucanthemum maximum*), Gerbera Daisy (*Gerbera jamesonii*), Lily of the Valley (*Convallaria majalis*), Rose, orange (*Rosa*), Honeysuckle (*Lonicera*), Hibiscus (*Hibiscus*), Meadowsweet (*Filipendula ulmaria*), Cowslip (*Primula veris*), Lime (*Tilia x europaea*), Golden Trumpet Tree (*Tabebuia alba*)

Harmony: Japanese Cherry (*Prunus serrulata*), Sweet Pea (*Lathyrus odoratus*), Meadowsweet (*Filipendula ulmaria*), Tiger Lily (*Lilium tigrinum*)

Healing: Blue Gum Flower (*Eucalyptus globulus*), Flannel Flower (*Actinotus helianthi*), Kangaroo Paw (*Anigozanthos manglesii*), Madonna Lily (*Lilium candidum*), Tree Peony (*Paeonia suffruticosa*), Rose, pale pink (*Rosa*), Self-heal (*Prunella vulgaris*), Dandelion (*Taraxacum officinale*), Feverfew (*Tanacetum parthenium*), Meadowsweet (*Filipendula ulmaria*)

Higher learning: African Violet (*Saintpaulia*)

Honesty: Chrysanthemum, White (*Chrysanthemum*), Rose, White (*Rosa*), Daphne (*Daphne odora*), Honesty (*Lunaria annua*)

Honour: Lily (*Lilium*), Peony (*Paeonia officinalis*), Wisteria (*Wisteria sinensis*), Speedwell (*Veronica officinalis*)

Hope: Jasmine (*Jasminum officinale*), Poet's Narcissus (*Narcissus poeticus*), Snowdrop (*Galanthus nivalis*), Freesia (*Freesia*),

Daffodil (*Narcissus pseudonarcissus*), Hawthorn (*Crataegus monogyna*), Star of Bethlehem (*Ornithogalum*), Bee Balm (*Monarda*), Easter Lily (*Lilium longiflorum*), Columbine (*Aquilegia vulgaris*), Rose, Cherokee (*Rosa laevigata*), Iris, German (*Iris germanica*)

Humility: Buttercup (*Ranunculus acris*), Lilac (*Syringa vulgaris*), Lily of the Valley (*Convallaria majalis*), Sweet Violet (*Viola odorata*)

I

Ideas, new: Indian Paintbrush (*Castilleja miniata*), Mock Orange (*Philadelphus*), Water Lily, White (*Nymphaea*)

Immortality: Ambrosia (*Ambrosia*), Periwinkle (*Vinca minor*), Myrtle (*Myrtus*), Yew (*Taxus baccata*), Peach Blossom (*Prunus persica*)

Immunity: Pansy (*Viola tricolor var. hortensis*), Echinacea (*Echinacea purpurea*)

Independence: Common Thistle (*Cirsium vulgare*), Geraldton Wax (*Chamelaucium uncinatum*), Everlasting Daisy (*Rhodanthe chlorocephala*), Nasturtium (*Tropaeolum majus*), Sea Holly (*Eryngium maritimum*)

Inner strength: Dahlia (*Dahlia*), Wild Pansy (*Viola tricolor*), Snapdragon (*Antirrhinum majus*), Scotch Thistle (*Onopordum acanthium*), Thistle, Common (*Cirsium vulgare*)

Innocence: Baby's Breath (*Gypsophila paniculata*), Chrysanthemum, White (*Chrysanthemum*), Shasta Daisy (*Leucanthemum maximum*), Freesia (*Freesia*), Lily of the Valley (*Convallaria majalis*), Daphne (*Daphne odora*), Orange Blossom (*Citrus x sinensis*), Star of Bethlehem (*Ornithogalum*), Easter Lily (*Lilium longiflorum*), Stargazer Lily, White (*Lilium orientalis*)

Insight: Speedwell (*Veronica officinalis*), Eyebright (*Euphrasia officinalis*), Evening Primrose (*Oenothera*), California Pitcher Plant (*Darlingtonia californica*), Lilac, White (*Syringa*)

Inspiration: Siberian Iris (*Iris sibirica*), Daffodil (*Narcissus pseudonarcissus*), Iris, Blue Flag (*Iris versicolor*)

Integrity: Royal Bluebell (*Wahlenbergia gloriosa*), Echinacea (*Echinacea purpurea*), Thistle, Scotch (*Onopordum acanthium*), Chinese Plum (*Prunus mume*)

Intelligence: Dandelion (*Taraxacum officinale*), Ginger (*Zingiber officinale*)

Intimacy: Flannel Flower (*Actinotus helianthi*), Honeysuckle (*Lonicera spp.*), Tuberose (*Polianthes tuberosa*), Purslane (*Portulaca oleracea*)

Intuition: Queen of the Night (*Selenicereus grandiflorus*), Angel's Trumpet (*Brugmansia candida*), Speedwell (*Veronica officinalis*)

Invitation: Chrysanthemum, Red (*Chrysanthemum spp.*)

J

Jest: Nasturtium (*Tropaeolum majus*), Celosia (*Celosia*)

Joy: Golden Wattle (*Acacia pycnantha*), Chrysanthemum,

Florist's (*Chrysanthemum morifolium*), Hollyhock (*Alcea rosea*), Daphne (*Daphne odora*), Hibiscus (*Hibiscus spp.*), Orange Blossom (*Citrus x sinensis*)

Justice: Black-Eyed Susan (*Rudbeckia hirta*)

K

Keep going: Geraldton Wax (*Chamelaucium uncinatum*)

Keep your promise: Plum (*Prunus domestica*)

Kindness: Primrose (*Primula vulgaris*)

Kiss me: Mistletoe (*Viscum album*), Love-in-a-Mist (*Nigella damascena*)

Know, I: Angel's Trumpet (*Brugmansia candida*)

Knowledge: Cornflower (*Centaurea cyanus*), Anemone (*Anemone*), Water Lily, Pink (*Nymphaea*), Water Lily, Blue (*Nymphaea*)

L

Lasting affection: Kalanchoe (*Kalanchoe spp.*)

Last forever, I wish this moment would: Everlasting Daisy (*Rhodanthe chlorocephala*)

Leadership: Delphinium (*Delphinium*), Jack-in-the-pulpit (*Arisaema triphyllum*), Black Orchid (*Trichoglottis brachiata*)

Learning: Orange Banksia (*Banksia ashbyi*), Lime (*Tilia x europaea*), African Violet (*Saintpaulia spp.*)

Letting go: Angel's Trumpet (*Brugmansia candida*), Bleeding Heart (*Lamprocapnos spectabilis*)

Life-force: Carnation (*Dianthus caryophyllus*), Marigold (*Tagetes erecta*)

Life purpose: Wedding Bush (*Ricinocarpos pinifolius*), Edelweiss (*Leontopodium alpinum*), Lily of the Valley (*Convallaria majalis*)

Limits: Rhododendron (*Rhododendron spp.*)

Longevity: Chrysanthemum, Florist's (*Chrysanthemum morifolium*), Wisteria (*Wisteria sinensis*), Bouvardia (*Bouvardia spp.*)

Longing for you: Camellia, Pink (*Camellia*)

Love: Carnation (*Dianthus caryophyllus*), Native Passion Flower (*Passiflora herbertiana*), Apple Blossom (*Malus domestica*), Chrysanthemum, Red (*Chrysanthemum spp.*), Rose, Red (*Rosa spp.*), Daphne (*Daphne odora*), Meadowsweet (*Filipendula ulmaria*), Love-in-a-Mist (*Nigella damascena*), Cosmos (*Cosmos spp.*), Wisteria (*Wisteria sinensis*), Columbine (*Aquilegia vulgaris*), Morning Glory (*Ipomoea purpurea*), Water Lily, Red (*Nymphaea*), Lovage (*Levisticum officinale*), Chamomile, German (*Matricaria chamomilla*), Sweet Violet (*Viola odorata*), Myrtle (*Myrtus*), Iris, German (*Iris germanica*), Geranium (*Geranium*), Michaelmas Daisy (*Aster amellus*), Patchouli (*Pogostemon cablin*), Ylang-Ylang (*Cananga odorata*), Jacaranda (*Jacaranda acutifolia*), Hibiscus, Red (*Hibiscus rosa-sinensis*)

Luck, good: Carnation, White (*Dianthus caryophyllus*), Heather, Lavender (*Calluna vulgaris*), Bells of Ireland (*Moluccella laevis*), Centaury (*Erythraea centaurium*), Elder (*Sambucus nigra*), Red Clover (*Trifolium pratense*), Clover (*Trifolium*)

Lust: Oleander (*Nerium oleander*), Rose, Red (*Rosa*), Water Lily, Red (*Nymphaea*)

M

Magick: Mistletoe (*Viscum album*), Yew (*Taxus baccata*) Marigold (*Tagetes erecta*), Rose, Mauve (*Rosa spp.*), Foxglove (*Digitalis purpurea*), Opium Poppy (*Papaver somniferum*)

Magnificence: Bird of Paradise (*Strelitzia reginae*), Calla Lily (*Zantedeschia aethiopica*)

Marriage: Mistletoe (*Viscum album*), Orange Blossom (*Citrus x sinensis*), Lemon Verbena (*Aloysia triphylla*), Myrtle (*Myrtus spp.*)

Meet me?, will you: Scarlet Pimpernel (*Anagallis arvensis*)

Memories: Forget-me-not (*Myosotis spp.*)

Memory: Field Poppy (*Papaver rhoeas*), Rosemary (*Rosmarinus officinalis*), Eyebright (*Euphrasia officinalis*)

Mirth: Crocus (*Crocus*), Scarlet Pimpernel (*Anagallis arvensis*)

Misunderstandings cleared: Yellow Jessamine (*Gelsemium sempervirens*)

Motherly love: Carnation, Pink (*Dianthus caryophyllus*), Impatiens (*Impatiens walleriana*)

Motivation: Self-heal (*Prunella vulgaris*), Black-Eyed Susan (*Rudbeckia hirta*)

Mourning: Weeping Willow (*Salix babylonica*), Bellflower (*Campanula spp.*)

Move on, let's: Lilac (*Syringa vulgaris*)

Mutual love: Ambrosia (*Ambrosia spp.*)

N

Needs, changing: Statice (*Limonium spp.*)

Negative emotions, clear: Gerbera Daisy, Orange (*Gerbera jamesonii*)

New home: Cornflower (*Centaurea cyanus*)

New ideas: Indian Paintbrush (*Castilleja miniata*), Mock Orange (*Philadelphus*), Water Lily, White (*Nymphaea*)

New love: Cornflower (*Centaurea cyanus*), Water Lily, Red (*Nymphaea spp.*)

New mother: Lily (*Lilium spp.*)

New opportunity: Delphinium (*Delphinium spp.*)

No: Chrysanthemum, Yellow (*Chrysanthemum*), Hemlock (*Conium maculatum*), Cyclamen (*Cyclamen*), Nightshade (*Solanaceae*), Carnation, Striped (*Dianthus caryophyllus*)

No one could love you more: Cosmos (*Cosmos spp.*)

Nobility: Peony (*Paeonia officinalis*)

Nurturing: Mock Orange (*Philadelphus*), Primrose (*Primula vulgaris*), Chickweed (*Stellaria media*), Elder (*Sambucus nigra*)

O

Openness: Ice Plant (*Carpobrotus edulis*), Lime (*Tilia x europaea*), Trilobed Violet (*Viola palmata*)

Opportunity: Rosella Flower (*Hibiscus heterophyllus*), Delphinium (*Delphinium*)

Optimism: Golden Wattle (*Acacia pycnantha*), Anemone (*Anemone*), Chrysanthemum, Florist's (*Chrysanthemum morifolium*), Freesia (*Freesia*), Hollyhock (*Alcea rosea*)

P

Pain: Nettle (*Urtica spp.*), Rose, Cherokee (*Rosa laevigata*)

Pain, let go of: Crocus (*Crocus spp.*)

Pain, pleasure mixed with: Dog Rose (*Rosa canina*)

Painful memories: Pheasant's Eye (*Adonis vernalis*)

Passion: Red Tulip (*Tulipa*), Waratah (*Telopea speciosissima*), Tulip, Wild (*Tulipa sprengeri*), Chrysanthemum, Red (*Chrysanthemum*), Rose, Red (*Rosa spp.*), Passion Flower (*Passiflora incarnata*), Trillium (*Trillium spp.*), Water Lily, Red (*Nymphaea*), Hibiscus, Red (*Hibiscus rosa-sinensis*)

Passionate love: Bleeding Heart (*Lamprocapnos spectabilis*)

Path, life: African Daisy (*Osteospermum*)

Patience: Scottish Primrose (*Primula scotica*), Aster (*Aster spp.*), Forsythia (*Forsythia spp.*), Primrose (*Primula vulgaris*), Chamomile, Roman (*Chamaemelum nobile*), Wisteria (*Wisteria sinensis*), Michaelmas Daisy (*Aster amellus*), Ox-eye Daisy (*Leucanthemum vulgare*)

Peace: Billy Buttons (*Pycnosorus globosus*), Japanese Cherry (*Prunus serrulata*), California Poppy (*Eschscholzia californica*), Honesty (*Lunaria annua*), Apple Blossom (*Malus domestica*), Camellia, Japanese (*Camellia japonica*), Meadowsweet (*Filipendula ulmaria*), Cosmos (*Cosmos spp.*), Lilac, White (Syringa), Passionfruit (Passiflora edulis), Vanilla (Vanilla planifolia), Ylang-Ylang (Cananga odorata)

Perseverance: Hydrangea (*Hydrangea*)

Platonic love: Bittersweet (*Solanum dulcamara*), Acacia (*Acacia*)

Play: Hyacinth (*Hyacinthus*)

Playfulness: Daisy (*Bellis perennis*), African Daisy (*Osteospermum*), Canna (*Canna generalis 'Striatus'*)

Positive change: Edelweiss (*Leontopodium alpinum*), Dog Rose (*Rosa canina*)

Possibilities: Crowea (*Crowea exalata*), Himalayan Blue Poppy (*Meconopsis grandis*), Delphinium (*Delphinium*)

Power: Violet Nightshade (*Solanum brownii*), Queen of the Night (*Selenicereus grandiflorus*), Dandelion (*Taraxacum officinale*), Jonquil (*Narcissus jonquilla*)

Pride: Amaryllis (*Amaryllis spp.*), Lily (*Lilium spp.*), Heliconia (*Heliconia spp.*), African Daisy (*Osteospermum spp.*), Thistle, Scotch (*Onopordum acanthium*), Hop (*Humulus lupulus*), Tiger Lily (*Lilium tigrinum*), Texas Bluebonnet (*Lupinus texensis*), Auricula (*Primula auricular*)

Priorities: Petunia (*Petunia spp.*)

Proud of you, I am: Tiger Lily (*Lilium tigrinum*), Lily (*Lilium spp.*), Heliconia (*Heliconia spp.*)

Progression: Five Corners (*Styphelia laeta*), Carnation (*Dianthus caryophyllus*), Hibiscus, White (*Hibiscus arnottianus*), Crepe Myrtle (*Lagerstroemia indica*)

Promise, I: Madonna Lily (*Lilium candidum*), Chrysanthemum, White (*Chrysanthemum*)

Prosperity: Tree Peony (*Paeonia suffruticosa*), Peruvian Lily (*Alstroemeria*), Peony (*Paeonia officinalis*), Peach Blossom (*Prunus persica*), Great Rhododendron (*Rhododendron maximum*), Queen of the Meadow (*Filipendula ulmaria*)

Protection: Daisy (*Bellis perennis*), Lavender (*Lavandula stoechas*), Sweet Pea (*Lathyrus odoratus*), Delphinium (*Delphinium*), Queen Anne's Lace (*Daucus carota*), Rose, White (*Rosa*), Tuberose (*Polianthes tuberosa*), Delphinium (*Delphinium*), Galangal (*Alpinia galangal*), St John's Wort (*Hypericum perforatum*), Calendula (*Calendula officinalis*), Petunia (*Petunia*), Garlic (*Allium sativum*), Hellebore (*Helleborus*)

Pure, our love is: Rose, Lavender (*Rosa spp.*)

Purification: Hawthorn (*Crataegus monogyna*), Feverfew (*Tanacetum parthenium*), Hyssop (*Hyssopus officinalis*), Iris, Blue Flag (*Iris versicolor*), Yellow Jessamine. (*Gelsemium sempervirens*)

Purity: Baby's Breath (*Gypsophila paniculata*), Carnation, White (*Dianthus caryophyllus*), Chrysanthemum, White (*Chrysanthemum*), Rose, White (*Rosa*), Dogwood (*Cornus*), Easter Lily (*Lilium longiflorum*), Stargazer Lily, White (*Lilium orientalis*), Water Lily (*Nymphaea*), Camellia, White (*Camellia*), Lilac, White (*Syringa*), Mexican Orange Blossom (*Choisya ternata*)

Q

Quick decision: Iris Croatica (*Iris perunika*)

Quickly, leave me: Pennyroyal (*Mentha pulegium*)

Quiet, be: Belladonna (*Atropa belladonna*)

R

Rare beauty: Hibiscus, Pink (*Hibiscus rosa-sinensis*)

Rashness: Hyacinth (*Hyacinthus*)

Ready for you, I am: Venus Flytrap (*Dionaea muscipula*)

Ready, I am: Pelargonium *(Pelargonium cucullatum*), Rosella Flower (*Hibiscus heterophyllus*)

Rebirth: Crowfoot (*Erodium crinitum*), Sacred Blue Lily (*Nymphaea caerulea*), Dogwood (*Cornus*), Dagger's Log (*Agave karatto* Miller)

Recognition: Amaryllis (*Amaryllis spp.*)

Rejuvenation: Calla Lily (*Zantedeschia aethiopica*)

Release: Calendula (*Calendula officinalis*), Rose, Meadow (*Rosa blanda*)

Remembrance: Forget-me-not (*Myosotis spp.*), Pansy (*Viola tricolor var. hortensis*), Easter Lily (*Lilium longiflorum*), Rosemary (*Rosmarinus officinalis*)

Renewal: Marigold (*Tagetes erecta*), Snowdrop (*Galanthus nivalis*), Daffodil (*Narcissus pseudonarcissus*)

Resignation: Cyclamen (*Cyclamen*), Harebell (*Campanula rotundifolia*)

Resilience: Dahlia (*Dahlia spp.*), Elder (*Sambucus nigra*)

Resolution: Crowea (*Crowea exalata*), Rose, Musk (*Rosa moschata*)

Respect: Oleander (*Nerium oleander*), Hibiscus, White (*Hibiscus arnottianus*), Rose, Red (*Rosa*), Daffodil (*Narcissus pseudonarcissus*)

Responsibility: Violet Nightshade (*Solanum brownii*)

Romance: Carnation (*Dianthus caryophyllus*), Azalea (*Rhododendron subgenus Tsutsusi*), Peony (*Paeonia officinalis*)

S

Sacrifice: Field Poppy (*Papaver rhoeas*)

Sacredness: Sacred Blue Lily (*Nymphaea caerulea*), Calendula (*Calendula officinalis*)

Sad memories: African Daisy (*Osteospermum spp.*)

Safety: Borage (*Borago officinalis*), Baby Blue Eyes (*Nemophila menziesii*)

Sanctuary: Queen Anne's Lace (*Daucus carota*)

Secret: Woodbine (*Lonicera periclymenum*), Ranunculus (*Ranunculus*), Gardenia (*Gardenia jasminoides*), Madonna Lily (*Lilium candidum*)

Self-confidence: Sunflower (*Helianthus annuus*), Suncup (*Lonicera ovata*)

Self-improvement: Tulip, Wild (*Tulipa sprengeri*)

Self-love: Orchid (*Orchidaceae*), Poet's Narcissus (*Narcissus poeticus*)

Self-worth: Calla Lily (*Zantedeschia aethiopica*)

Sex: Orchid (*Orchidaceae spp.*), Tuberose (*Polianthes tuberosa*), Ylang-Ylang (*Cananga odorata*)

Silence: Belladonna (*Atropa belladonna*)

Sincerity: Rose, Dark Pink (*Rosa*), Honesty (*Lunaria annua*)

Sorry, I am: Flannel Flower (*Actinotus helianthi*), Scottish Primrose (*Primula scotica*), Rose, pale pink (*Rosa*), Rose, Musk (*Rosa moschata*), Calendula (*Calendula officinalis*), Snapdragon (*Antirrhinum majus*)

Spirituality: African Violet (*Saintpaulia spp.*)

Stability: Shasta Daisy (*Leucanthemum maximum*), *Passion* Flower (*Passiflora incarnata*)

Stay true: Azalea (*Rhododendron subgenus Tsutsusi*)

Strength: Rosella Flower (*Hibiscus heterophyllus*), Magnolia (*Magnolia campbellii*), Peruvian Lily (*Alstroemeria*), Sunflower (*Helianthus annuus*), Tuberose (*Polianthes tuberosa*)

Success: Acacia (*Acacia*), *Melissa* (*Melissa officinalis*), Iris, Fairy (*Dietes grandiflora*), Baby Blue Eyes (*Nemophila menziesii*), Flame Lily (*Gloriosa rothschildiana*)

Survival: Waratah (*Telopea speciosissima*), Dandelion (*Taraxacum officinale*), Texas Bluebonnet (*Lupinus texensis*)

Support: Daisy (*Bellis perennis*)

Sweetness: Lily of the Valley (*Convallaria majalis*), Daphne (*Daphne odora*)

Sympathy: Shasta Daisy (*Leucanthemum maximum*), Statice (*Limonium*)

T

Take care of yourself: Azalea (*Rhododendron subgenus Tsutsusi*)

Taste, good: Fuchsia (*Fuchsia magellanica*)

Tell me the truth: Chrysanthemum, White (*Chrysanthemum*)

Thank you: Poinsettia (*Euphorbia pulcherrima*), Bluebell, Common (*Hyacinthoides non-scripta*), Rose, Dark Pink (*Rosa*), Canterbury Bells (*Campanula medium*)

Thinking of you, I am: Heartsease (*Viola tricolor*)

This must end: Angel's Trumpet (*Brugmansia candida*), Begonia (*Begonia spp.*)

Transformation: Evening Primrose (*Oenothera spp.*)

Trust: Lavender (*Lavandula stoechas*), Rose, Wild (*Rosa acicularis*), Freesia (*Freesia*), Heather, White (*Calluna vulgaris*), Chrysanthemum, White (*Chrysanthemum*)

Truth: Lily (*Lilium*), Rose, White (*Rosa*), Thistle, Scotch (*Onopordum acanthium*), Iris Croatica (*Iris perunika*)

U

Unconditional love: Scottish Primrose (*Primula scotica*), Straw Flower (*Xerochrysum bracteatum*), Chicory (*Cichorium intybus*)

Understanding: Boronia (*Boronia ledifolia*), Camellia, Japanese (*Camellia japonica*), Hydrangea (*Hydrangea*), Calendula (*Calendula officinalis*)

Undying love: Purple Tulip (*Tulipa spp.*)

Unfeeling, you are: Hydrangea (*Hydrangea*)

Unity: Water Lily (*Nymphaea*), Honeysuckle (*Lonicera*), Tiger Lily (*Lilium tigrinum*)

Unrequited love: Daffodil (*narcissus pseudonarcissus*), Dogwood (*Cornus spp.*)

V

Valour: Iris, Blue Flag (*Iris versicolor*), Iris, Black (*Iris nigricans*), Iris, German (*Iris germanica*)

Victory: Jasmine (*Jasminum officinale*)

Vigour: Marigold, Mexican (*Tagetes erecta*), Nasturtium (*Tropaeolum majus*), Lemon Balm (*Melissa officinalis*), Elder (*Sambucus nigra*)

Vitality: Marigold (*Tagetes erecta*), Dahlia (*Dahlia spp.*), Lilac (*Syringa vulgaris*), *Daffodil* (*Narcissus pseudonarcissus*), Nasturtium (*Tropaeolum majus*), *Morning* Glory (*Ipomoea purpurea*)

W

Want you, I: Tulip, Wild (*Tulipa sprengeri*)

War: Yarrow (*Achillea millefolium*), Tansy (*Tanacetum vulgare*)

Warmth: Dandelion (*Taraxacum officinale*)

Warning: Canterbury Bells (*Campanula medium*), Begonia (*Begonia*)

Wealth: Peruvian Lily (*Alstroemeria*), Peony (*Paeonia officinalis*), Pink Stargazer Lily (*Lilium orientalis*)

Welcome: Flamingo Flower (*Anthurium*), Rose, Yellow (*Rosa spp.*)

Well, get: Sunflower (*Helianthus annuus*)

Will you marry me?: Wedding Bush (*Ricinocarpos pinifolius*)), Honey Grevillea (*Grevillea eriostachya*), Rose, Wild (*Rosa acicularis*), Lisianthus (*Eustoma grandiflorum*), Blushing Bride (*Tillandsia ionantha*), Mistletoe (*Viscum album*), Orange Blossom (*Citrus x sinensis*), Myrtle (*Myrtus*), Queen of the Meadow (*Filipendula ulmaria*)

Wisdom: Magnolia (*Magnolia campbellii*), Water Lily, Blue (*Nymphaea*), Iris, Blue Flag (*Iris versicolor*), Jacaranda (*Jacaranda acutifolia*)

Wishes: Heather, White (*Calluna vulgaris*), Dandelion (*Taraxacum officinale*), Iris, Fairy (*Dietes grandiflora*)

Y

Yes: Golden Wattle (*Acacia pycnantha*), Carnation, Red (*Dianthus caryophyllus*)

Youth: Frangipani (*Plumeria alba*), Foxglove (*Digitalis purpurea*), Hibiscus (*Hibiscus*), Primrose (*Primula vulgaris*), Marguerite Daisy (*Argyranthemum frutescens*), Lilac, White (*Syringa*), Hibiscus, Red (*Hibiscus rosa-sinensis*)

Z

Zeal: Lords and Ladies (*Arum maculatum*)

Zest: Lemon (*Citrus limon*)

Flowers of the Month

You may like to select flowers to match the birth month of a person or that align with the month of an event you are planning.

Traditional Western Culture Flowers of the Month

January: Carnation (*Dianthus caryophyllus*), Snowdrop (*Galanthus nivalis*)

February: Primrose (*Primula scotica*), Iris (*Iris*)

March: Daffodil (*narcissus pseudonarcissus*)

April: Shasta Daisy (*Leucanthemum maximum*), Daisy (*Bellis perennis*)

May: Lily (*Lilium*), Lily of the Valley (*Convallaria majalis*)

June: Rose (*Rosa*)

July: Waterlily (*Nymphaea*), Sweet Pea (*Lathyrus odoratus*), Delphinium (*Delphinium*)

August: Gladiolus (*Gladiolus*)

September: Aster (*Aster*)

October: Dahlia (*Dahlia*), Marigold (*Tagetes erecta*)

November: Chrysanthemum (*Chrysanthemum*)

December: Holly (*Ilex aquifolium*), Poinsettia (*Euphorbia pulcherrima*)

Chinese Flowers of the Month

January: Plum Blossom (*Prunus mume*)

February: Peach Blossom (*Prunus persica*)

March: Tree Peony (*Paeonia suffruticosa*)

April: Cherry Blossom (*Prunus serrulata*)

May: Magnolia (*Magnolia campbellii*)

June: Pomegranate (*Punica granatum*)

July: Lotus (*Nelumbo nucifera*)

August: Pear Blossom (*Pyrus*)

September: Mallow Blossom (*Malva sylvestris*)

October: Chrysanthemum (*Chrysanthemum*)

November: Gardenia (*Gardenia jasminoides*)

December: Poppy (*Papaver rhoeas*)

Japanese Flowers of the Month

January: Pine (*Pinus*)

February: Plum Blossom (*Prunus mei*)

March: Cherry Blossom (*Prunus serrulata*), Peach Blossom (*Prunus persica*), Pear Blossom (*Pyrus*)

April: Cherry Blossom (*Prunus serrulata*), Wisteria (*Wisteria sinensis*)

May: Azalea (*Rhododendron subgenus Tsutsusi*), Peony (*Paeonia officinalis*)

June: Iris (*Iris*)

July: Morning Glory (*Ipomoea purpurea*), Mountain Clover (*Trifolium montanum*)

August: Lotus (*Nelumbo nucifera*)

September: Seven Grasses of Autumn – Hagi Bush: Japanese Clover (*Lespedeza*), Susuki: Pampas Grass (*Cortaderia selloana*), Kuzu: Arrowroot (*Maranta arundinacea*), Nadeshiko: Wild Carnation (*Dianthus*), Ominaeschi: Maiden Flower (*Patrinia scabiosifolia*), Fujibakama: Chinese Agrimony (*Agrimonia pilosa*), Hirogao: Wild Morning Glory (*Ipomoea*)

October: Maple (*Acer*), Chrysanthemum (*Chrysanthemum*)

November: Maple (*Acer*), Willow (*Salix alba*)

December: Camellia (*Camellia japonica*), Empress Tree (*Paulownia tomentosa*)

Australian Flowers of the Month

January: Billy Buttons (*Pycnosorus globosus*)

February: Blue Gum Flower (*Eucalyptus globulus*)

March: Orange Banksia (*Banksia ashbyi*)

April: Tea Tree (*Leptospermum myrsinoides*)

May: Crowea (*Crowea exalata*)

June: Geraldton Wax (*Chamelaucium uncinatum*)

July: Gymea Lily (*Doryanthes excelsa*)

August: Waratah (*Telopea speciosissima*)

September: Golden Wattle (*Acacia pycnantha*)

October: Flannel Flower (*Actinotus helianthi*)

November: Kangaroo Paw (*Anigozanthos manglesii*)

December: Rosella Flower (*Hibiscus heterophyllus*)

Flowers of the Zodiac

Aquarius

20th January ~ 18th February

Snowdrop (*Galanthus nivalis*), Foxglove (*Digitalis purpurea*), Mullein (*Verbascum Thapsus*), Orchid (*Orchidaceae*), Gentian (*Gentiana*)

Pisces

19th February ~ 20th March

Violet (*Viola*), Carnation (*Dianthus caryophyllus*), Heliotrope (*Heliotropium*) Opium Poppy (*Papaver somniferum*), Peruvian Lily (*Alstroemeria*)

Aries

21st March ~ 19th April

Gorse (*Ulex europaeus*), Holly (*Ilex aquifolium*), Nasturtium (*Tropaeolum majus*), Scotch Thistle (*Onopordum acanthium*), Common Thistle (*Cirsium vulgare*), Tulip (*Tulipa*), Wild Rose (*Rosa acicularis*), Woodbine (*Lonicera periclymenum*)

Taurus

20th April ~ 20th May

Apple (*Malus domestica*), Cherry (*Prunus serrulata*), Coltsfoot (*Tussilago farfara*), Lily (*Lilium*), Lily of the Valley (*Convallaria majalis*), Lovage (*Levisticum officinale*), Violet (*Viola*), Wild Rose (*Rosa acicularis*), Almond (*Prunus amygdalus*), Ash (*Fraxinus*)

Gemini

21st May ~ 20th June

Dill (*Anethum graveolens*), Iris (*Iris*), Rose (*Rosa*), Parsley

(*Petroselinum crispum*), Snapdragon (*Antirrhinum majus*), Hazel (*Corylus*)

Cancer

21st June ~ 22nd July

Delphinium (*Delphinium*), Honesty (*Lunaria annua*), Moonwort (*Botrychium lunaria*), Poppy (*Papaver rhoeas*), Waterlily (*Nymphaea*), Rose, White (*Rosa*), Willow (*Salix alba*), Agrimony (*Agrimonia eupatoria*)

Leo

23rd July ~ 22nd August

Angelica (*Angelica archangelica*), Borage (*Borago officinalis*), Cowslip (*Primula veris*), Forsythia (*Forsythia*), Heliotrope (*Heliotropium*), Hops (*Humulus*), Laurel (*Laurus nobilis*), Marigold (*Tagetes erecta*), Peony (*Paeonia officinalis*), Sunflower (*Helianthus annuus*)

Virgo

23rd August ~ 22nd September

Cornflower (*Centaurea cyanus*), Daisy (*Leucanthemum maximum, Bellis perennis*), Madonna lily (*Lilium candidum*), Rosemary (*Rosmarinus officinalis*), Valerian (*Polemonium caeruleum*)

Libra

23rd September ~ 22nd October

Almond (*Prunus amygdalus*), Apple (*Malus domestica*), Hydrangea (*Hydrangea*), Love-in-a-Mist (*Nigella damascena*), Plum (*Prunus domestica*), Violet (*Viola*), Rose, White (*Rosa*)

Scorpio

23rd October ~ 21st November

Basil (*Ocimum basilicum*), Chrysanthemum (*Chrysanthemum*), Heather (*Calluna vulgaris*), Holly (*Ilex aquifolium*), Celandine (*Ficaria verna*), Peony (*Paeonia officinalis*)

Sagittarius

22nd November ~ 21st December

Carnation (*Dianthus caryophyllus*), Mulberry (*Morus*), Sage (*Salvia officinalis*), Wallflower (*Erysimum*)

Capricorn

22nd December ~ 19th January

Holly (*Ilex aquifolium*), Nightshade (*Solanaceae*), Rue (*Ruta graveolens*), Snowdrop (*Galanthus nivalis*), Solomon's Seal (*Polygonatum*), Violet (*Viola*), Yew (*Taxus baccata*)

Anniversary Flowers

1st Carnation (*Dianthus caryophyllus*)

2nd Lily of the Valley (*Convallaria majalis*)

3rd Sunflower (*Helianthus annuus*)

4th Hydrangea (*Hydrangea*)

5th Daisy (*Leucanthemum maximum, Bellis perennis*)

6th Calla Lily (*Zantedeschia aethiopica*)
7th Freesia (*Freesia*)
8th Lilac (*Syringa vulgaris*)
9th Bird of Paradise (*Strelitzia reginae*)
10th Daffodil (*Narcissus pseudonarcissus*)
11th Tulip (*Tulipa*)
12th Peony (*Paeonia officinalis*)
13th Chrysanthemum (*Chrysanthemum*)
14th Orchid (*Orchidaceae*)
15th Rose (*Rosa*)
20th Aster (*Aster*)
25th Iris (*Iris*)
30th Lily (*Lilium*)
40th Gladiolus (*Gladiolus*)
50th Violet (*Viola*), Yellow Rose (*Rosa*)

Flowers of the Days of the Week

Sunday

California Poppy (*Eschscholzia californica*)

Chrysanthemum (*Chrysanthemum*)

Day Lily (*Hemerocallis*)

Sunflower (*Helianthus annuus*)

Marigold (*Tagetes erecta*)

Monday

Honesty (*Lunaria annua*)

Lily of the Valley (*Convallaria majalis*)

White Rose (*Rosa*)

Snowdrop (*Galanthus nivalis*)

Phlox (*Phlox*)

Tuesday

Nasturtium (*Tropaeolum majus*)

Geranium (*Geranium*)

Dahlia (*Dahlia*)

Red Hot Poker (*Kniphofia*)

Wednesday

Lupin (*Lupinus perennis*)

Columbine (*Aquilegia*)

Vervain (*Verbena officinalis*)

Thursday

Lilac (*Syringa vulgaris*)

Lavender (*Calluna vulgaris*)

Violet (*Viola*)

Stock (*Matthiola incana*)

Cyclamen (*Cyclamen*)

Friday

Forget-me-not (*Myosotis*)

Carnation (*Dianthus caryophyllus*)

Love-in-a-Mist (*Nigella damascena*)

Pink Rose (*Rosa*)

Saturday

Wallflower (*Erysimum*)

Chrysanthemum (*Chrysanthemum*)

Fuchsia (*Fuchsia magellanica*)

Dahlia (*Dahlia*)

About the Author

Cheralyn Darcey is a botanical explorer, florist, organic gardener, environmental artist and the author and illustrator of over a dozen botanical titles that share with readers her passion for nature and researching plants and their relationships with us. Living on the Central Coast of NSW, Australia, Cheralyn has created and nurtures her own extensive flower, vegetable and interesting plant home garden that has been featured in national publications and is her creative sanctuary.

For more information, visit:

Website: www.cheralyndarcey.com

Instagram: cheralyn

Youtube: Florasphere

Facebook: cheralyn.darcey

More titles in the series ...

The Gift of Dreams

ISBN 978-1-925017-83-0

The Gift of Spells

ISBN 978-1-925429-37-4

The Gift of Crystals

ISBN 978-1-925017-82-3

The Gift of Nature

ISBN 978-1-925682-27-4

Available at all good bookstores